Starting Your North Carolina Nonprofit

Richard Wayne Bobholz

ISBN: 9780997733853

DEDICATION

This guide is dedicated to all the nonprofits I've had the pleasure of working with. Thank you for all you do for the community and helping me learn and grow.

CONTENTS

INTRODUCTION TO FORMING YOUR NORTH CAROLINA NONPROFIT

Forming a North Carolina Nonprofit Corporation is actually easier than a lot of places make you think. This guide will take you through the steps. By the end, you'll have all the legal documents you need to set up your North Carolina Nonprofit.

In this guide, we're covering the following steps:

1. Name Search
2. Nonprofit Articles of Incorporation

3. EIN
4. Starter Nonprofit Bylaws
5. Conflict of Interest Policy
6. First Board Meeting
7. Tips for Moving Forward

Don't panic! This is a very long guide because there's a lot of information to go through. However, if you take it one step at a time, it's pretty easy! Feel free to take breaks and come back. There are also lots of linked articles in here to help with adjacent information. I had to pick and choose what content was necessary to include here in order to keep the guide a manageable size.

Disclaimers

Because I'm a lawyer, I need to put in a few disclaimers first.

This guide is intended to be educational in nature. This is not legal advice. You're not my client unless you and I sign an agreement that says you are. There's no attorney-client relationship or confidentiality unless and until we've both signed an engagement letter.

This is based on North Carolina law that was current as of the date this guide was published. If you're in another state, these laws may not apply to you. It is also possible the laws have changed since I updated this guide last.

Forming any company comes with a lot of risk. You're taking the risk on for yourself.

What You Need to Know

Before we can dive right in, we need to cover a few things.

First, nonprofit corporations are not businesses owned in the same way for-profit businesses are owned[1]. Technically, the state owns them and the board of directors manages them or delegates the management to officers.

Second, because of their ownership status, you can't buy or sell nonprofits.

Third, one of the biggest concepts in nonprofit law is the conflict of interest. You always have to avoid even the appearance of a conflict.

Fourth, there's a difference between a nonprofit and a charity[2]. A charity is an entity that has received public charity recognition through section 501(c)(3) of the Internal Revenue Code. Obtaining this recognition requires an application and an entire separate process.

Now that we covered the preliminary information, let's dive right in.

NAME SEARCH

The first tangible legal step towards forming your North Carolina Nonprofit is the name search. When you conduct a name search, you're basically trying to figure out (1) if your desired name is already in use and (2) if you are infringing on anyone's trademark rights.

Naming Guidelines

Firstly, you need to make sure you're following the Naming Guidelines for North Carolina Companies[3]. You're not allowed to use certain words like "bank" or "engineer" without first getting approved by the proper legal authority.

Eliminating Potential Problems

Throughout this step, you're eliminating potential problems. You'll never be 100% certain that your name is available. There are just too many different ways someone could have accumulated rights in that name. For example, you're not going to be able to check your trademark in every language on the USPTO trademark search. Instead, you're just aiming to search the likely ones.

Secretary of State Name Availability

Our starting point is the North Carolina Department

of the Secretary of State's website. That's sosnc.gov. It's such a long name, most people call it the Secretary of State. To search name availability, go to https://sosnc.gov/online_services/search/by_title/_Business_Registration[4]. Their search will ignore disregarded words like "the" and "to." For example, if you want to form a company called "The Catskill Consulting Company," it will read "Catskill Consulting" to the Secretary of State based on the legal naming guidelines.

When you're checking the Secretary of State's website, you just need to make sure there's no other company that someone would confuse yours for. Generally, that's just a 1:1 match you're trying to avoid. However, I'd also recommend checking for any companies that share the same base portion of your name. Using the above example, "Catskill Consulting" as the base part, if there's a company called "Catskill Advising," that's probably too close for comfort and you'll want to pick a new name.

Alternatively, you can always reach out to the company you're in potential conflict with and see if they'll let you coexist or buy the name from them. Just because someone is using the name you want does not mean all hope is lost.

Numbers in Names

I've seen a lot of people create problems when they use numbers in their company name. Company names are not like email addresses. If someone already has "Catskill Consulting," you cannot name your company "Catskill Consulting 2." It would pass the Secretary of State's checks, but it would be an unlawful name unless you're the one who owns "Catskill Consulting."

Searching the Secretary of State's website should only take you about 5-15 minutes depending on how similar your company name is to others.

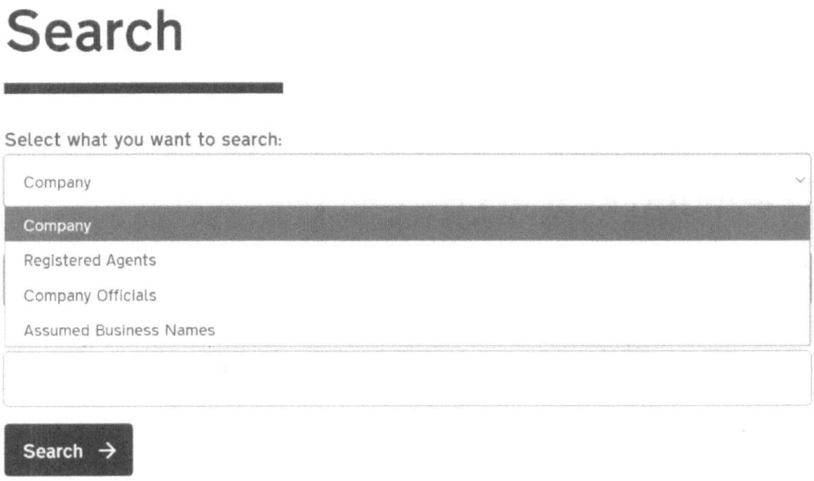

Screenshot of the "select what you want to search" dropdown menu on the secretary of state's name search page.

Assumed Name Availability

Next, it is time to search assumed names[5]. Assumed Names, as they're legally called in North Carolina, are often referred to as DBAs, fictitious names, or "also known as" names. Whatever you call them, they're when you call your company anything besides its legal name. For example, "Law Plus Plus" is an assumed name for "R. W. Bobholz Law, PLLC".

To search assumed names, we actually go to the same place as the Secretary of State name search. Fortunately, you just need to run through the same process as before and you're good to go.

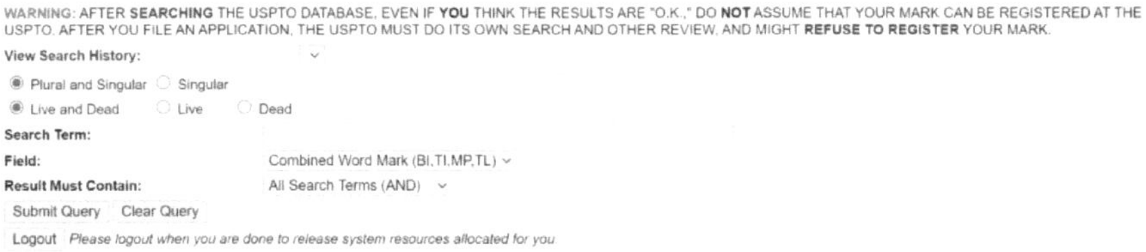

Screenshot of the trademark search fields on uspto.gov.

Trademark Search

Now we're on the hardest part of the name search. In this step, you're searching the Federal trademarks[6] to see if there are any filed marks someone could confuse for your own. There are actually a lot of considerations during this part, so let's explore them.

In order to violate someone else's trademark, your name must be (1) similar enough to cause confusion and (2) in the same industry. If you don't satisfy both of those criteria, there's no conflict. The standard is "likelihood of confusion" for whether or not a name infringes on someone's trademark. It doesn't have to be an exact match.

Also, merely descriptive company names[7] cannot be trademarked, so if you have a table making company in Durham called “Durham Table Makers Inc,” you couldn’t trademark that anyway, so there’s no point in doing a trademark search on that name.

This is one area where it helps to have an extra opinion. I find a lot of business owners find reasons why the trademarks they find are not close enough. An objective set of eyes helps.

Exact Match

Firstly, head over to the trademark search tool and type in your desired name exactly as it would appear. If nothing comes up with the exact match, move on to the next step.

If you get just one result, the search tool will bring you to that trademark specifically. Check to see if your industry conflicts with any of their industries. If there’s no overlap, you’re probably good to move on.

More likely, you’re going to see a list of results. It’s time to go through every single live one and see if there’s (1) overlap in industry and (2) likelihood of confusion in the mark. For example, “landslide” returns 36 results. Of those, only 13 are live. One of the live ones is “306 TO 223. LANDSLIDE,SHELLACKIN” whatever that means. If you’re registering “landslide” as a type of coffee, you don’t have to worry about that weird one above.

Common Replacements

Secondly, you need to search your desired company name with common replacements. For example, sometimes people use the letter 8 inside of words that rhyme with "ate," like "L8r." The USPTO will not do this search for you. They will search Arabic numerals and written numbers as the same thing when they're a separate word, but not when they're within a word. For example, you'll need to search both "later" and "l8r" in the above example.

Core Part

In addition to searching your company name as a whole, you also need to search just the core piece. For example, if your company's name is Achilles Motorcycles & Racetrack Repair," you need to see if "Achilles" or "Achilles Motorcycles" would infringe on anyone's trademark. Remember, the standard is "likelihood of confusion" so if people would think you're a subsidiary of another company, that's potential for infringement.

Different Languages

In our "landslide" example above, you'd also have to test out other languages. Fortunately, USPTO is in English, so they require other marks be translated to English so that everyone can compare to the same language. In that landslide example, "Reliz Creek" came up. "Reliz" means "Landslide" in Spanish.

If, however, your company's name will be in a language other than English, you'll have to check the English form of the word.

However, I would not rely on the USPTO always returning the results for foreign languages. Therefore, you should search some of the more common languages when you're doing your search, especially for the core parts of your mark.

State Trademark Search

Because I know you haven't had enough fun searching databases yet, it's time to do the trademark search again, but using North Carolina's Trademark Search[8]. Conduct this search the same way as you did the federal search.

Just to make sure you're fully covered, you should also search the state trademarks for any state you're going to have a substantial presence in. Unfortunately, you don't have to be aware of someone else's trademark to infringe on it. And, the Secretary of State will not search any trademark office for you before registering your company.

Therefore, even if you're super diligent, you could still get in trouble for trademark infringement without ever knowing you were doing it. The best way to protect yourself is through a great search and then registering your company's name as a trademark with the USPTO 3-6 months after you start. A registered federal trademark will provide a lot of protection against future infringement claims against you.

Google Search

We're on the easier steps now. For this step, all you need to do is search your desired company's name in your favorite search engine and see what comes up. You're looking for the following:

1. Does it look like someone should have a trademark on this?
2. Is there a bad meaning or bad press behind the name I'm planning on using?
3. How much competition will I have using this name online?

I actually had one client refuse this step once because she thought that Google would steal her idea. I couldn't convince her that was ridiculous, so she registered her name without this step. Nothing bad happened (as far as I know), but I have to assure you that no one at Google is reviewing every single search query sent in. That's just an insane amount of work.

Domain Name Search

If you're looking for conspiracy theories, this is the step where they somewhat come true. I've put this one really low on the list because you want to check nearly everything else first. If your desired name has come through clean on every other step, it is time to see if you can get the domain.

Once you find a domain, you need to buy it. For example, if you're looking at PaintCoveredOveralls.com for your company's website, don't search it, add to cart, and then come back in a couple days. Some domain selling sites will actually charge you more if they notice a domain is getting a lot of attention.

In my opinion, it is better to buy a domain and not use it than to miss out on the domain you initially wanted. For my own businesses, I tend to buy several domains because I'm not sure which one I'll end up using. When it comes time for renewal, I just let the unused ones lapse.

Social Media

Finally, make sure you can get the handles you want for all the social media platforms. You don't even need to use them anytime soon. Just claim them and fill in the "about" section at some point. It costs you nothing to claim them, so it's a good idea to just do it.

Name Search Conclusion

That was a lot, right? Performing a name search for

your company is not a super quick and easy process. However, it is important that it is done right. That's why I tried to include as much information and examples as I could. Once you've done your search and are happy with the results, it's time to move on to the Articles of Incorporation.

In my opinion, the name search is the most legally grey area of starting a nonprofit. Once you've made it through this section, the rest will be a breeze.

ARTICLES OF INCORPORATION

Next up, it is time to draft and file our Nonprofit Articles of Incorporation. A template is included in the Exhibits section in the back of this book. You can also download a copy of this template at https://nc.business/product/nonprofit-articles-of-incorporation/.

Once you've downloaded our sample, we're going to walk through each piece individually. The North Carolina Secretary of State also has its own articles[9] you can use to set up your Nonprofit. However, mine are customized so that your nonprofit will be ready for potential 501c3 recognition from the IRS. If you file the ones from the Secretary of State, you will have to amend them when you apply for 501c3.

Name

You've done a ton of work checking to make sure your name is valid and available to be filed. You just have to put that chosen name on the line in section 1 of the articles.

Charitable or Religious Corporation

Next, if you're planning on going for 501c3 status, or are a church, check this box in section 2.

Registered Agent

Let's talk about registered agents[10]. Every business registered with the Secretary of State in North Carolina is required to have a registered agent. Their job is incredibly specific. All they're legally required to do is accept lawsuits and governmental notices on behalf of a company and forward those to the nonprofit's management.

The reason registered agents exist is so that people in North Carolina who deal with your company can always provide notice of lawsuits to a company. The state wants to ensure that a company cannot wrong consumers and then disappear. It's part of the tradeoff with these limited liability[11] entities like LLCs and corporations.

If a registered agent does not accept a lawsuit or important governmental notice, the sending party may serve the Secretary of State's office directly, and that still counts as notice for lawsuits and other proceedings. Therefore, if you don't have a reliable registered agent, you can be sued, lose, and never know you were sued in the first place.

To make matters even worse, if the Secretary of State gets served, the clerks there will attempt to contact you and also begin dissolving your company. If you don't stop the process, you might lose your nonprofit altogether.

Now that you know all that, you need to pick a

registered agent. It can really be any person or entity with a physical address in North Carolina who is responsible enough to let you know if you get sued. You can list yourself as well. Just make sure you don't take any super long vacations.

If you ever switch registered agents, make sure you update with the Secretary of State. Nonprofits aren't required to file annual reports, so you don't need to reverify every year.

Members

I've already marked that you don't have members. 99% of nonprofits don't have members. Even if you have members in your organization, they may not legally be members like this part is asking. In this case, members would be people who can vote to change the organization. Professional organizations, homeowners associations[12], and co-ops have members like this part is asking.

Distribution of Assets Upon Dissolution

I wouldn't recommend changing this section at all. Either keep it or delete it. It is a necessary clause if you're looking to become a 501c3 charity in the future. Otherwise, this clause isn't necessary. I've used this language many times, and it has been approved by the IRS every time.

Basically, this clause states what is legally required

anyway. Any funds or assets you have remaining if you dissolve your 501c3 charity must go to other 501c3 charities or to the state. That's because the money was given for charitable purposes and must remain as such or revert to the state.

No Benefit to Members and Directors

This is another clause that is only necessary if you're looking to become a 501c3 charity in the future. Either keep or delete this one as well. I wouldn't recommend making any changes because the IRS has accepted this language as is.

Regardless of if you have this clause or not, you have the same legal obligation outlined in this provision. Basically, you can't give equity, dividend, or payment of profits to members, directors, or officers except for reasonable compensation like wages.

That said, the IRS wants to see this policy in your articles if you're applying for 501c3 recognition. That's why it's included in my sample articles.

Conflicts of Interest Policy

The conflicts of interest policy isn't absolutely necessary, but I find it is helpful to have this portion in your articles. You'll need a more comprehensive one regardless. However, this is a good start. We'll cover what else to put in a conflicts of interest policy further down.

Conflicts of interest[13] arise when a director or officer is at odds with a decision they have to make. It becomes a problem when one potential decision benefits themselves. For example, if a director has the option to vote on whether or not to hire his company for a project for the nonprofit, that director has a conflict of interest.

Principal Office

North Carolina law requires that Nonprofit corporations list a principal office location in their articles of incorporation. The Principal Office can be the same as your registered agent as long as you're actually based there. If you list a registered agent that isn't you, but has the same address as the principal office address, this raises a red flag in the Secretary of State's office.

You do not need a principal office phone number listed.

Officers

Although this part is optional, it is very helpful for banking purposes. Some banks can handle articles without officers listed, but some cannot. It's an easy step to avoid hassles at the bank. You really only need 1 officer listed. I left you blanks for others, but you can feel free to delete the rows you don't use.

The downside to listing officers is having to change them with the Secretary of State's office. Because nonprofits don't have to file annual reports, you have to amend your filing every time you update your officers.

Effective Date

You don't have to list an effective date if you don't want to. If you leave it blank, the effective date will be the day you filed. You cannot list an effective date earlier than when you filed. I've only ever used this with for profit companies that want to avoid an additional annual report, so they list their effective date as January 1 of the next year. There's not much use for nonprofits unless you have a special day in mind.

Sign & Date

Finally, we need to sign and date the articles. You would think this is an easy step, but it's one of the most common reasons articles get rejected.

Date. The date is the date you are signing. That one is easy enough.

Incorporator Business Entity. You should never need to include an Incorporator Business Entity Name. This line exists solely for companies that mass file a bunch of articles like LegalZoom. They put LegalZoom on that line. You leave it blank.

Signature. Next, sign your legal name.

Print Name. Finally, type your legal name prior to the ", Incorporator". Do not list any other title. Again, companies that file these in bulk have another title. You do not.

Once you've signed and dated it, scan in a copy or save a signed copy in .pdf form to your computer where you can find it later. You're allowed to scan in a wet/ink signature or simply sign electronically with a stylus. Neither method has caused me any troubles in the past. Just keep track of where you saved your signed copy. We'll need it shortly.

Setting Up SOSNC.gov Account

You can always file by mailing in your articles or hand delivering them, but online is so much easier. Their office also handles online filing faster than in person, and I often get my approved articles faster than the mail would even deliver them.

To sign up for an account, go to https://www.sosnc.gov/online_services/account/register and fill in the requested information. There are actually very few required fields.

Drop down menu on secretary of state's website.

Filing Articles

Filing your articles is also a pretty easy step. Once logged into sosnc.gov, select "Create a Business Online" from the "I Want To..." dropdown menu, as shown in the picture above or go to this address: https://www.sosnc.gov/online_services/business_registration/flow_upload_a_filing

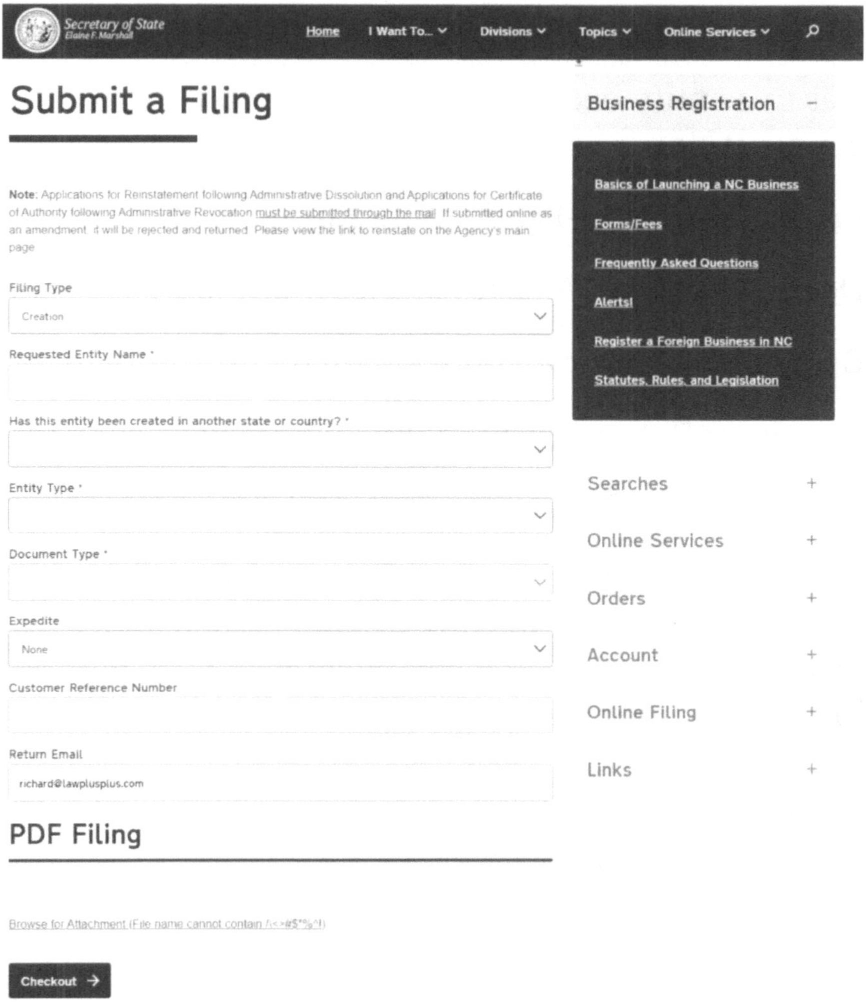

Create a business online page of the secretary of state's website.

Your page should look like the above image with the header "Submit a Filing." If not, try the link or menu again to get to that page. On this page, complete the information as follows:

Filing Type: Creation.

Requested Entity Name: Your desired company

name that you have listed on your articles.

Has this entity been created in another state or country? No.

Entity Type: Non-Profit Corporation

Document Type: Articles of Incorporation

Expedite: No, unless you want to. It costs more.

Customer Reference Number: leave blank

Return Email: Put your own email here.

Then, click "Browse for Attachment" hyperlink and upload the scanned in copy of your signed and dated articles. Once you've uploaded it, click Submit to go to the next screen.

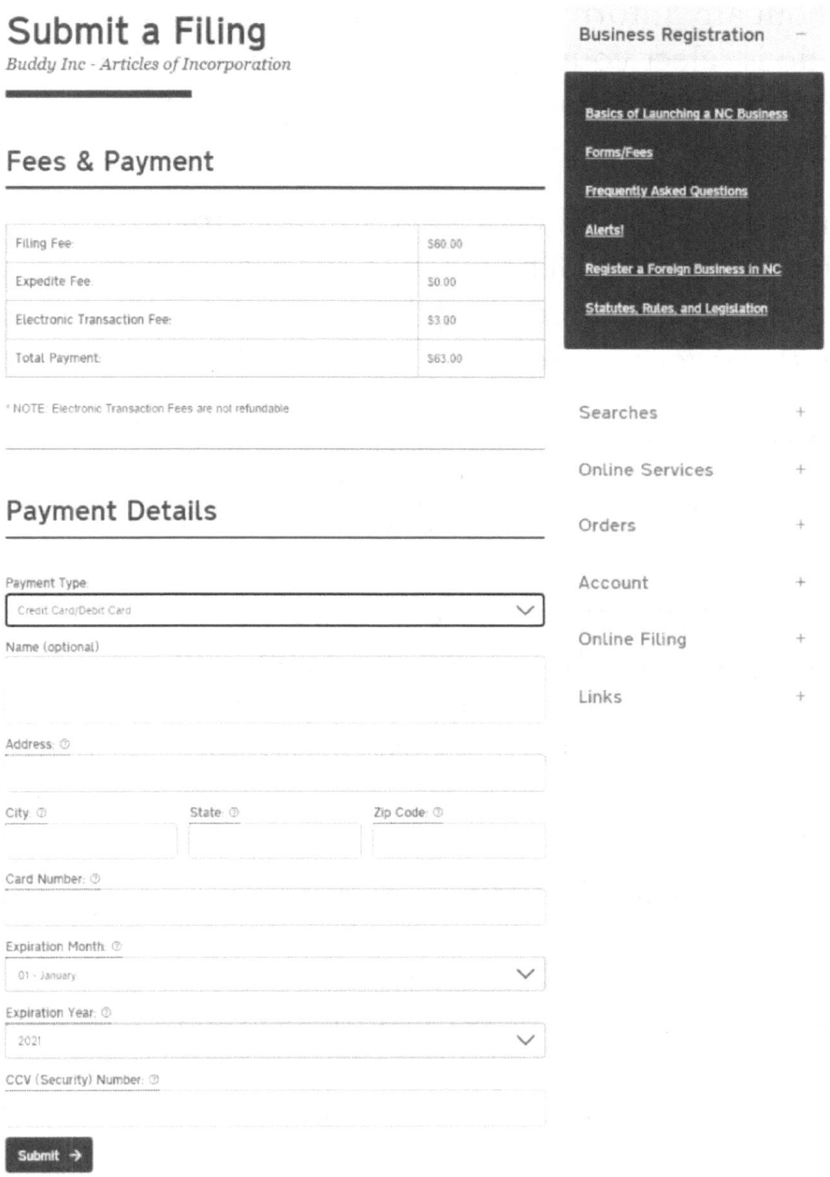

Submit a Filing

Buddy Inc - Articles of Incorporation

Fees & Payment

Filing Fee:	$60.00
Expedite Fee:	$0.00
Electronic Transaction Fee:	$3.00
Total Payment:	$63.00

* NOTE: Electronic Transaction Fees are not refundable

Payment Details

Payment Type:

Credit Card/Debit Card

Name (optional)

Address:

City:

State:

Zip Code:

Card Number:

Expiration Month:

01 - January

Expiration Year:

2021

CCV (Security) Number:

Submit →

Business Registration −

Basics of Launching a NC Business

Forms/Fees

Frequently Asked Questions

Alerts!

Register a Foreign Business in NC

Statutes, Rules, and Legislation

Searches +

Online Services +

Orders +

Account +

Online Filing +

Links +

Payment screen for filing a nonprofit articles of incorporation

Payment Screen

This is the second of two screens where you have to

fill out any information. On this screen, all you have to do is select your payment type and pay. Filing a Nonprofit corporation costs $63 unless you've selected to expedite your return.

Once you fill in all your payment information and click Submit, you'll be taken to the receipt page. I recommend downloading the receipt just in case anything goes wrong.

If anything is incorrect with your articles or your name gets rejected[14], someone from the Secretary of State's office will email you to have you correct it. Fortunately, you won't have to go through the whole process again, and it won't cost you any additional money. I've also found that once you're in the emailing stage, things happen very quickly. I've had a clerk process my articles within 5 minutes of me emailing them back.

The Waiting Game

If you've submitted everything properly, all you can do now is wait to hear back. If the Secretary of State approves your articles, you will get an email with your certificate of registration and a pdf about avoiding scams. Once you get the approval email, you're ready to move onto the next step: the EIN. You shouldn't start that next step until you get your approval email in case your name gets rejected.

EIN

Your EIN is your tax identification number for your nonprofit. It is like a social security number for entities. The IRS links everything tax related to your EIN. There are a lot of companies out there that charge you an awful lot for obtaining an EIN[15] for you. It's not that much work and they're free. I highly recommend doing this step yourself[16].

At some point I guess I should mention EIN stands for Employer Identification Number, but it has nothing to do with whether you have employees or not.

Importantly, the IRS will let you obtain an EIN prior to filing your articles, but this is legally incorrect and also potentially costly if your name gets rejected.

How Do You Get an EIN?

Firstly, you need to go to the IRS's EIN portal at https://www.irs.gov/businesses/small-businesses-self-employed/apply-for-an-employer-identification-number-ein-online[17]. I find it much easier to Google search "IRS EIN" and click the IRS link that comes up. Do not use anything that isn't irs.gov.

Click Apply Online Now, but keep in mind this online system is only available between 7am and

10pm EST, for some reason. You'll get a few notices in the beginning, but then you click "Begin Application."

Type of Legal Structure

After you go through the warnings, you'll be asked what type of legal structure is applying for an EIN. In your case, you're going to click the "View Additional Types" at the bottom and click "Continue".

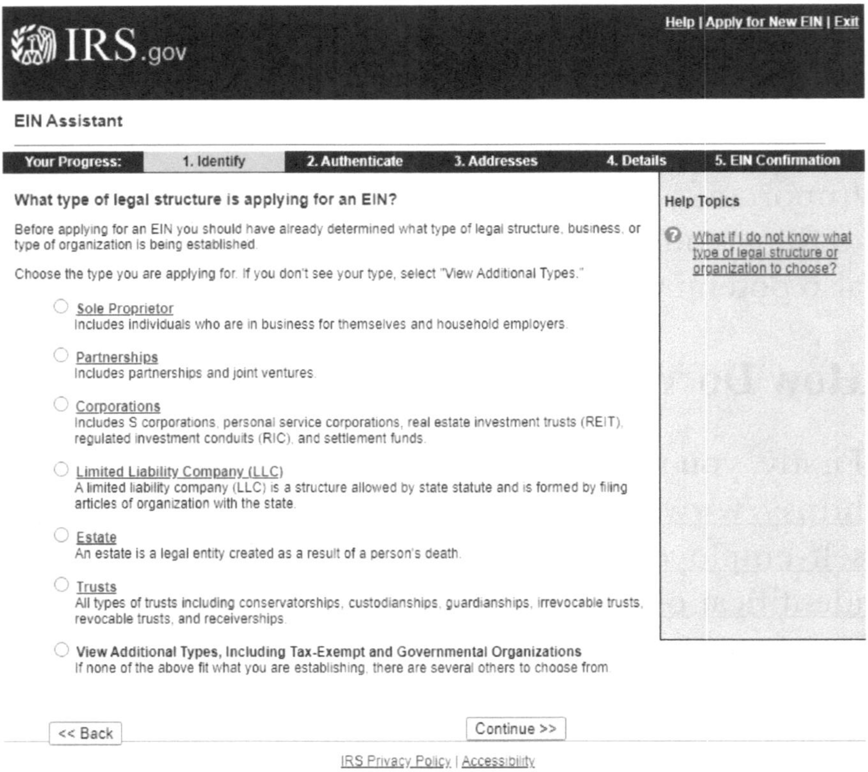

Types of legal structures on the IRS EIN application. Screenshot from irs.gov.

Next, select "Other Non-Profit Tax-Exempt Organizations" as seen below. I included the description of that category in the below screenshot for your reference.

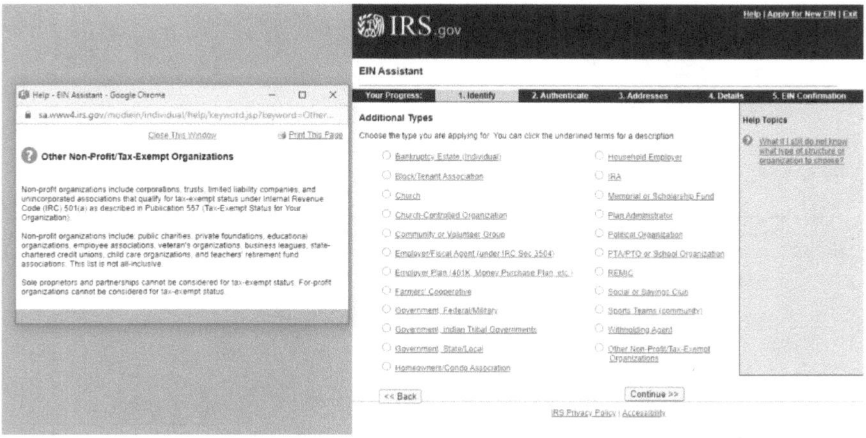

Additional legal entity types. Screenshot from irs.gov.

I like the IRS's online application process because they take the time to explain each step. The next screen you get after selecting your entity type is always an explanation and confirmation page. If you've selected "Other Non-Profit/Tax-Exempt Organizations," your next screen will look like the below screenshot.

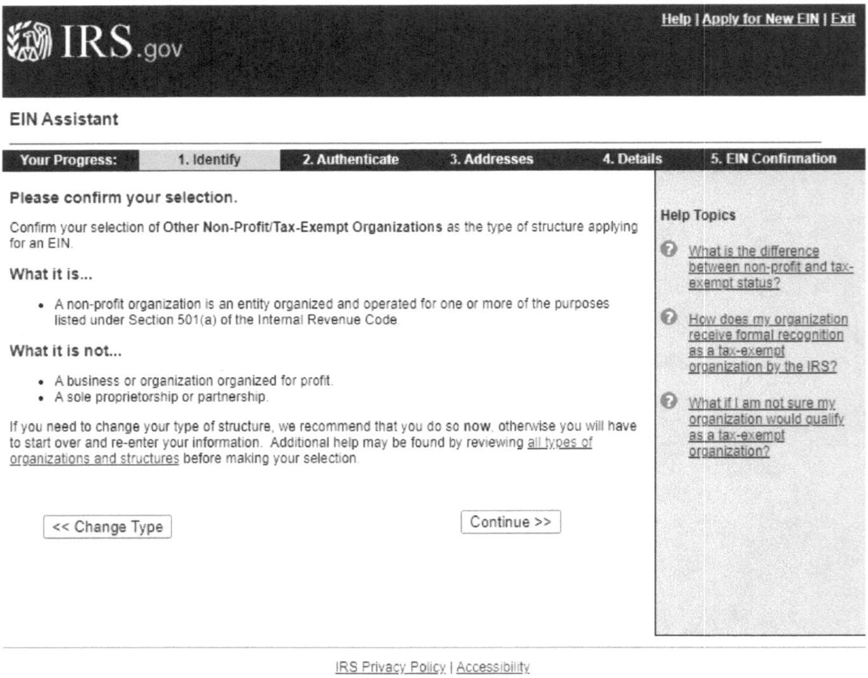

As you can see above, if you're applying for 501c3, this is the category for you.

Why Are You Requesting an EIN?

Next, the application wants to know why you are requesting an EIN. 99% of the time, I'm selecting "Started a new business." You don't need a new one if any of the other options happen. For example, if you hire employees in a couple years, you don't need a new EIN. Once you have one, you're good to go. That's the only EIN you'll need for your business.

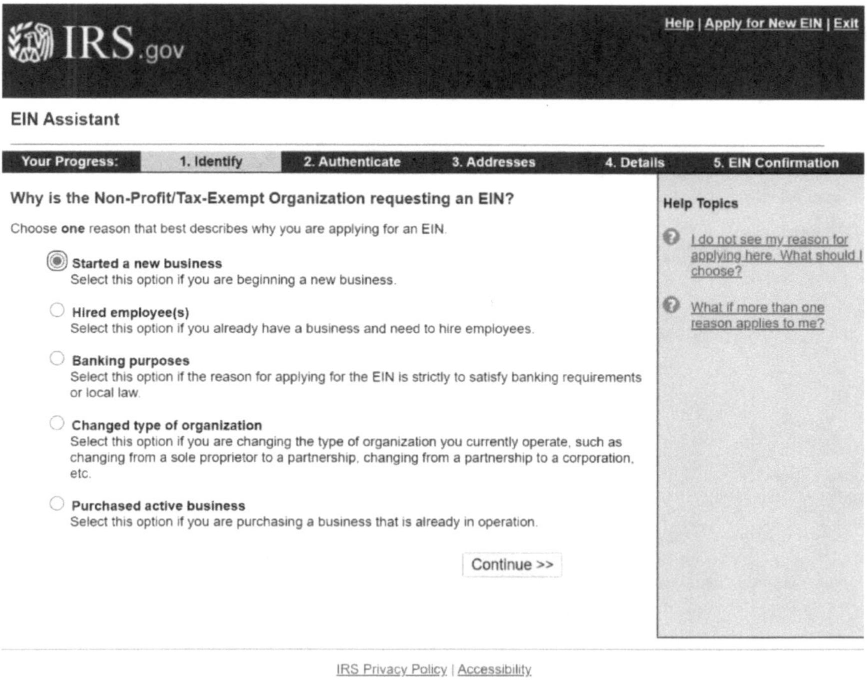

Reasons for requesting an EIN. Screenshot from irs.gov.

Responsible Party

The next section is the cause of most of the questions I field about EINs. The responsible party is just a person the IRS ties to the organization. They don't owe the taxes if the company can't pay. Instead, they're the person the IRS contacts if there is a tax problem.

Basically, everything in the IRS must eventually tie back to a real person. Therefore, the IRS wants a real person with their social security number named as the responsible party.

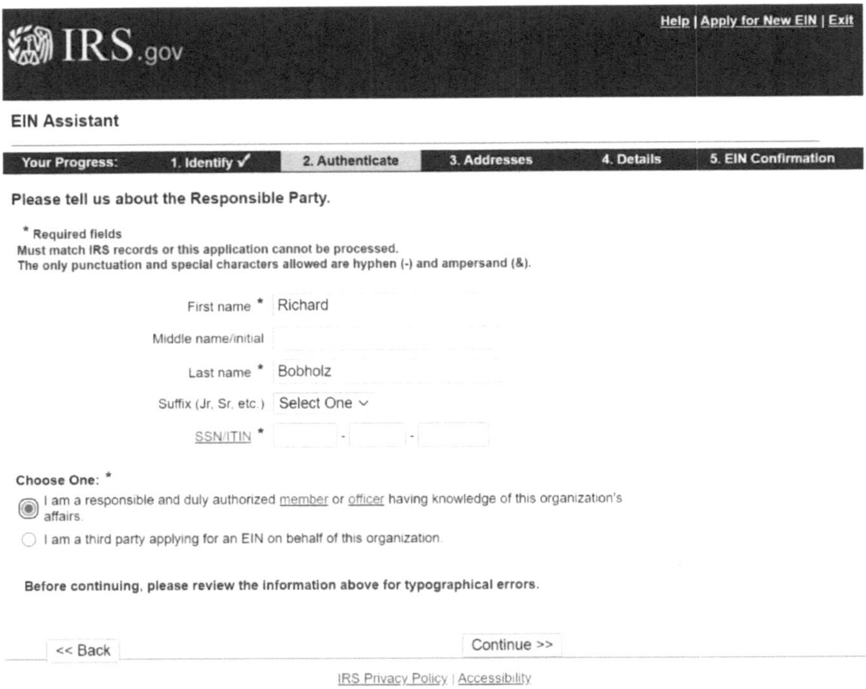
IRS.gov

Help | Apply for New EIN | Exit

EIN Assistant

Your Progress: 1. Identify ✓ 2. Authenticate 3. Addresses 4. Details 5. EIN Confirmation

Please tell us about the Responsible Party.

* Required fields
Must match IRS records or this application cannot be processed.
The only punctuation and special characters allowed are hyphen (-) and ampersand (&).

First name * Richard
Middle name/initial
Last name * Bobholz
Suffix (Jr, Sr, etc.) Select One
SSN/ITIN * - -

Choose One: *
I am a responsible and duly authorized member or officer having knowledge of this organization's affairs.
I am a third party applying for an EIN on behalf of this organization.

Before continuing, please review the information above for typographical errors.

<< Back Continue >>

IRS Privacy Policy | Accessibility

In your case, you're going to select that you're a responsible and duly authorized member or officer having knowledge of the organization's affairs.

Non-Profit Information

The next couple of screens ask for general information about the non-profit. If you have your filed Articles of Incorporation from above, you'll have all of this information right there.

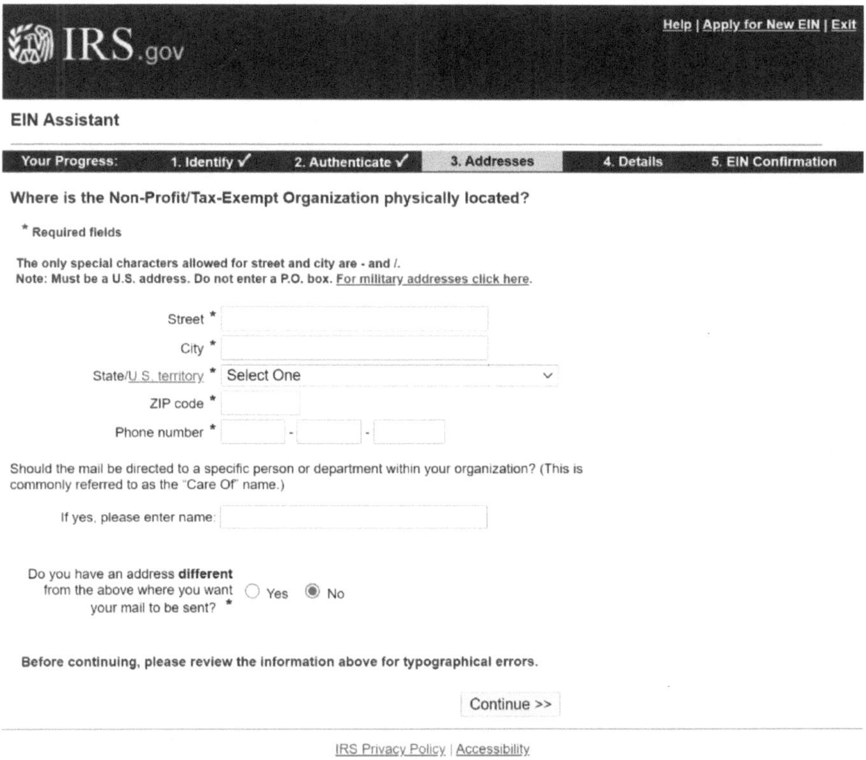

IRS.gov

Help | Apply for New EIN | Exit

EIN Assistant

Your Progress:	1. Identify ✓	2. Authenticate ✓	3. Addresses	4. Details	5. EIN Confirmation

Where is the Non-Profit/Tax-Exempt Organization physically located?

* Required fields

The only special characters allowed for street and city are - and /.
Note: Must be a U.S. address. Do not enter a P.O. box. For military addresses click here.

Street *

City *

State/U.S. territory * Select One

ZIP code *

Phone number * - -

Should the mail be directed to a specific person or department within your organization? (This is commonly referred to as the "Care Of" name.)

If yes, please enter name:

Do you have an address **different** from the above where you want your mail to be sent? * ○ Yes ◉ No

Before continuing, please review the information above for typographical errors.

Continue >>

IRS Privacy Policy | Accessibility

You do not need to list a trade name / doing business as name on the application unless you have one filed. A trade name's legal name in North Carolina is an assumed name[18].

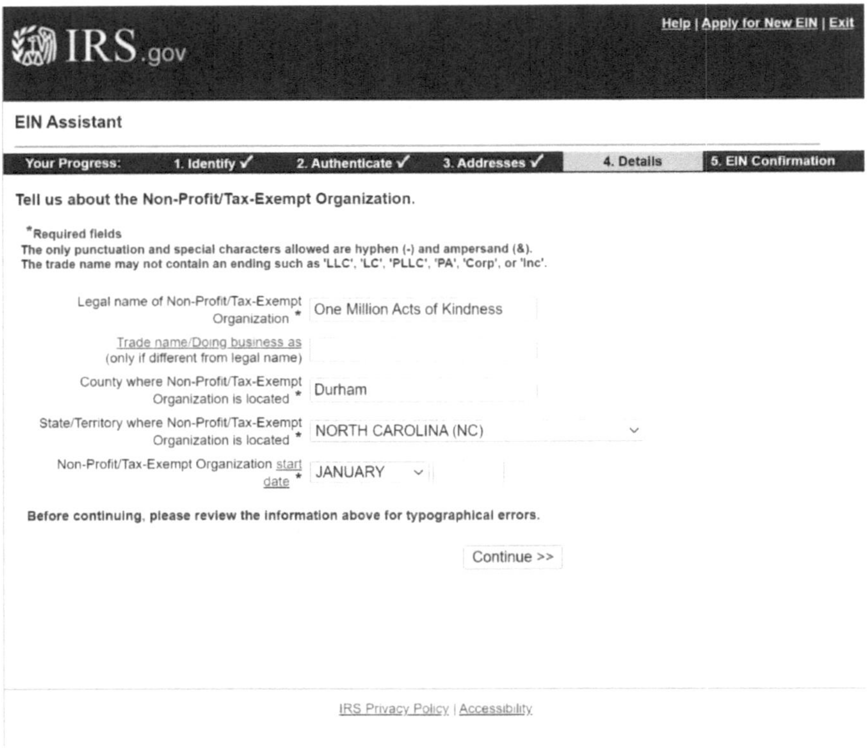

The No's Screen

I call the next screen the "No's Screen" because I regularly click no on all of them. However, if any of them apply to you, you should definitely check yes. For example, if you are starting with employees, you need to check yes on the bottom one.

However, if you're not sure if you'll have employees or not in the first 12 months, I recommend clicking no because this is one mechanism the IRS uses to catch fraud. If you click yes, but then don't have employees, they're going to follow up with you to see why you didn't do any withholdings. That's more work for you and the IRS.

Instead, once you do hire employees, you'll just set up the withholdings accounts and register your employees with the state.

On the other hand, if you do have employees from the start, checking yes here gives the IRS a heads up. They actually mail you information on withholding taxes to help you get started. And, it's pretty useful information!

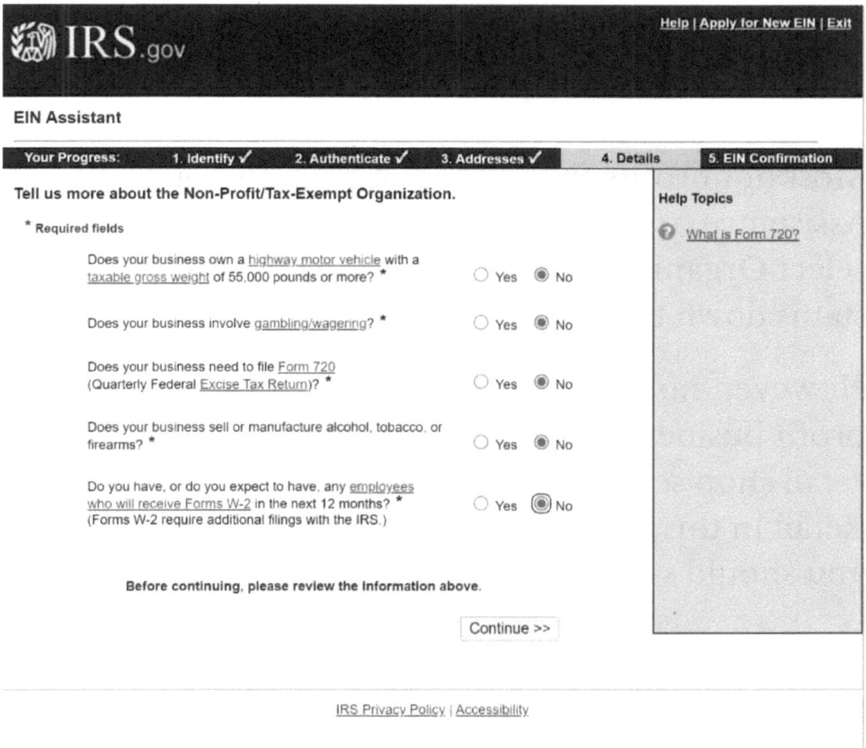

What Do You Do?

Finally, the IRS wants to know what you do as a

business. I'm still not 100% sure what they do with this information, but they want it.

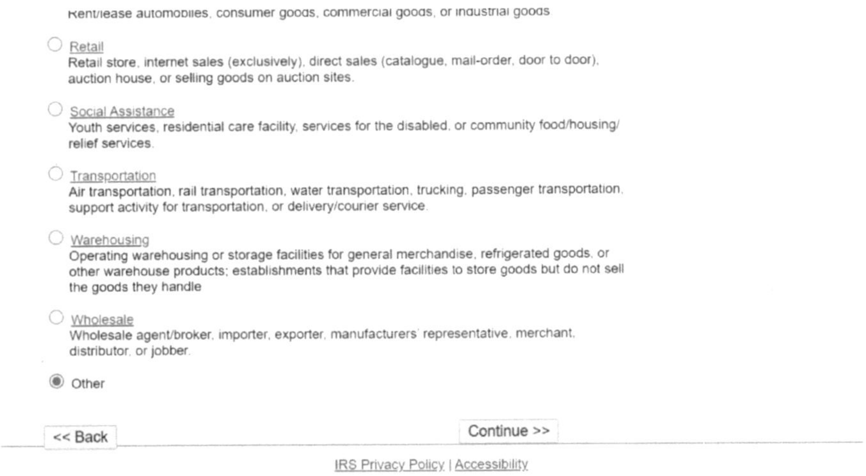
Rent/lease automobiles, consumer goods, commercial goods, or industrial goods

○ Retail
Retail store, internet sales (exclusively), direct sales (catalogue, mail-order, door to door), auction house, or selling goods on auction sites.

○ Social Assistance
Youth services, residential care facility, services for the disabled, or community food/housing/relief services.

○ Transportation
Air transportation, rail transportation, water transportation, trucking, passenger transportation, support activity for transportation, or delivery/courier service.

○ Warehousing
Operating warehousing or storage facilities for general merchandise, refrigerated goods, or other warehouse products; establishments that provide facilities to store goods but do not sell the goods they handle

○ Wholesale
Wholesale agent/broker, importer, exporter, manufacturers' representative, merchant, distributor, or jobber.

◉ Other

<< Back Continue >>

IRS Privacy Policy | Accessibility

Most nonprofits fit into one of two categories: Social Assistance or Other. In the Other category, you'd select Organization if you're trying to gain 501c3 status down the road.

However, nonprofits can do nearly anything a for profit business can do. For example, if you have a retail shop set up as a nonprofit, you should select Retail in this step. If you fit into multiple categories, you should select the primary activity.

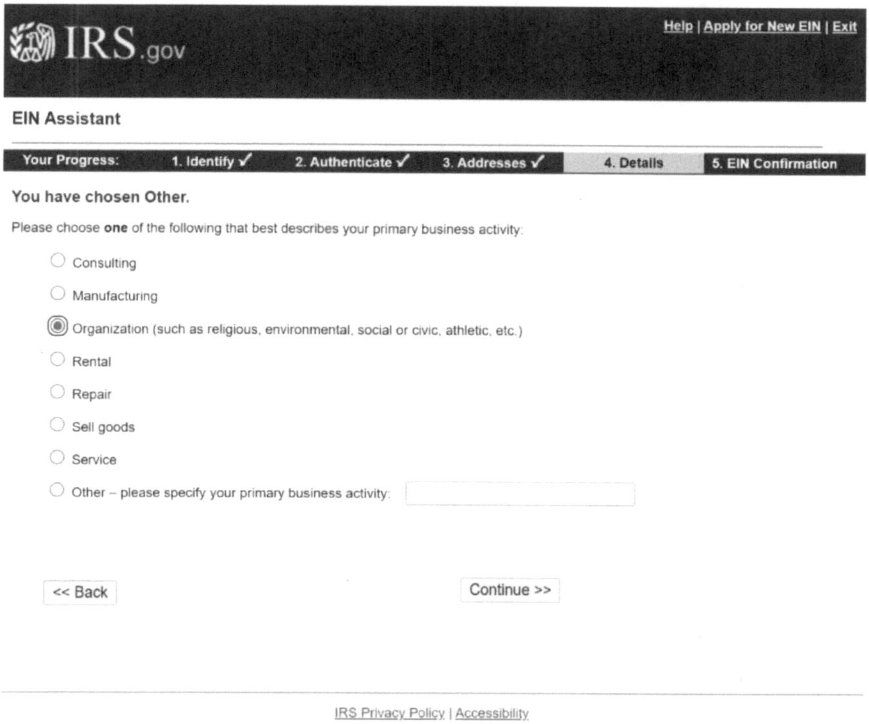

If you've selected Other and then Organization in the What Do You Do screens, you'll end up with the screen you see below. Pick whichever one fits best for what your organization provides. Keep in mind that "Other" is a perfectly safe option. A lot of organizations choose Other.

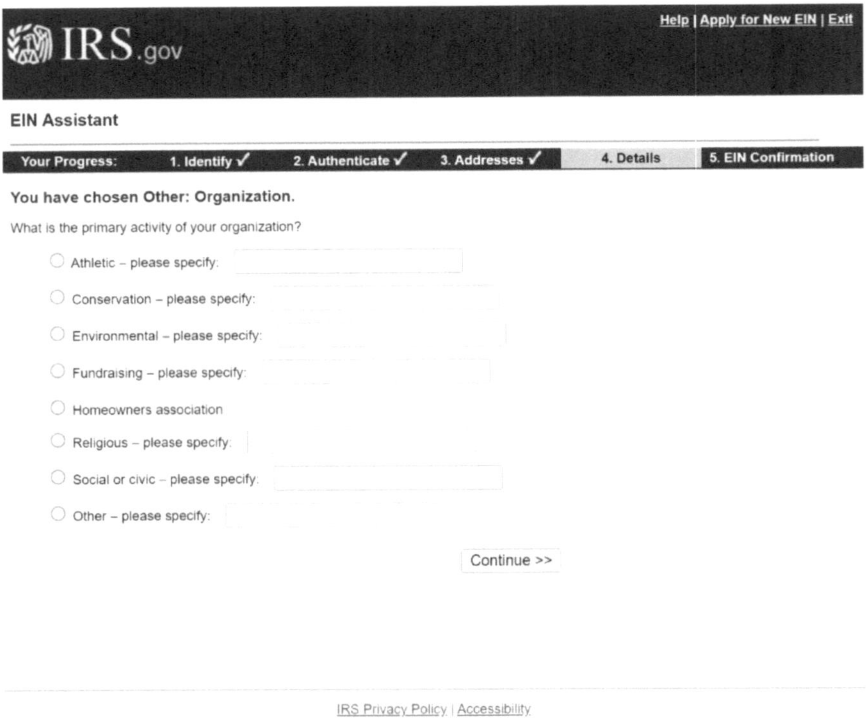

Get the PDF!

If you're obtaining the EIN on behalf of yourself, you get the option to get an EIN instantly. Take advantage of that. However, make sure you print off a copy and save this in multiple places. The IRS is really hard to work with to get a replacement EIN letter.

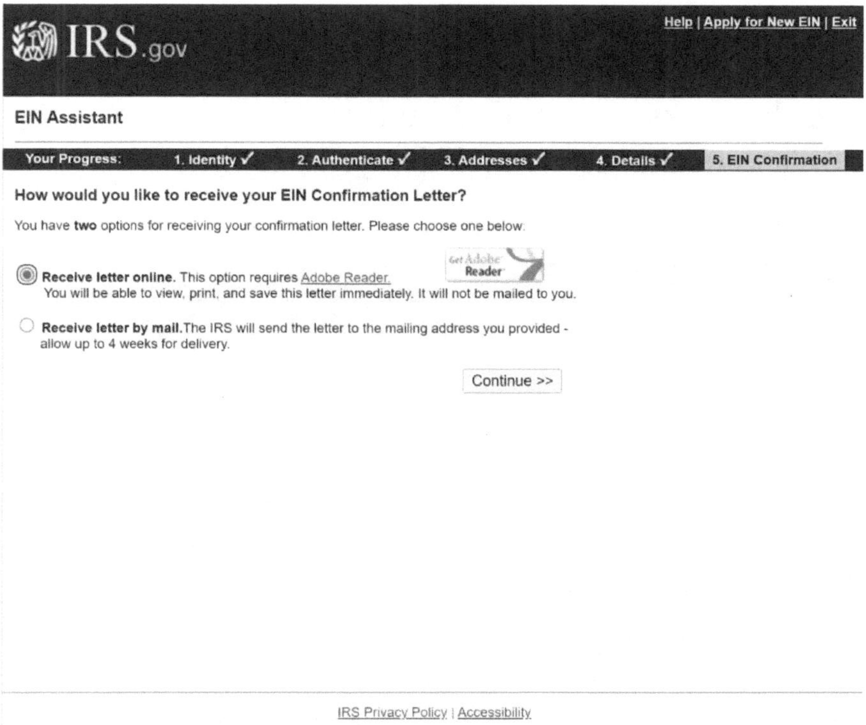

EIN delivery method page. Screenshot from irs.gov.

Review and Submit

If you've gone through all the previous steps and everything has worked out, you'll end up at the summary page. Double check that everything is entered correctly and hit Submit. It should only take a few seconds to reach the confirmation screen. You'll be asked to click a button to download the pdf of your EIN confirmation. I would recommend also taking a screenshot of the confirmation screen for your records.

When I formed my first company, the download

button had an error and I didn't get to download the EIN pdf. I still obtained a copy in the mail in a couple weeks, so it ended up fine. However, you don't want that stress and delay. Take that screenshot for proof.

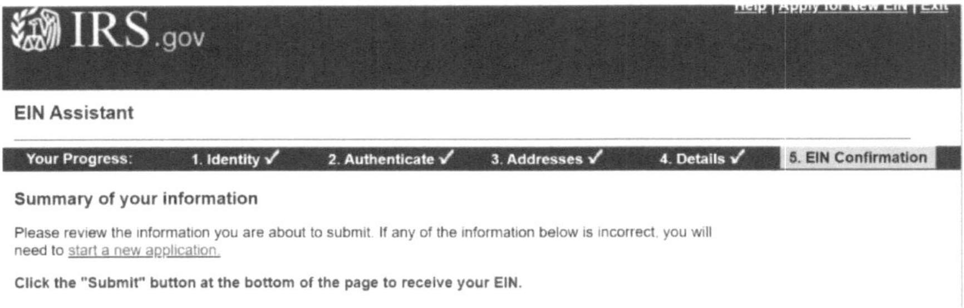

Congratulations! You now have an EIN for your business. You're getting very close to ready to take off running. All you have left are the bylaws, conflict of interest policy, board meeting, and solicitation license!

NONPROFIT BYLAWS

The next step is the creation of your Nonprofit Bylaws. A template of these bylaws is included in the exhibits of this book, or you can download a copy from the following address: https://nc.business/product/nc-nonprofit-bylaws/

Nonprofit bylaws are very different than for-profit bylaws. Whereas for-profit bylaws have to include a lot of information about ownership, stocks, and owner disputes, nonprofits don't have those same issues. This actually makes these bylaws relatively simple.

Regardless if you're using our template or not, all nonprofit bylaws need cover the following topics:

1. General Formation Information
2. Purpose
3. Board of Directors
4. Meeting Information
5. Executive Team
6. Legal Duties & Indemnity
7. Dissolution and Termination
8. General Formation Information

Starting off, it is important to identify the name and general information about your nonprofit. I always make the name the first section. That just makes it obvious who you're dealing with. That might be a product of dealing with hundreds of different companies.

This section is a good place for other generic information like how to amend the bylaws, what accounting method is used, and the state laws that apply. Your nonprofit bylaws are a "private" document. However, because it's a nonprofit, you still have to make them publicly available to certain organizations like the IRS and stakeholders that may need to see them. The content of this first section is really for those people.

Purpose

In this section, I like to list a general purpose, a specific purpose, and then any mission statements or non-discrimination policies. It's a fairly straightforward section with minimal legalese. For your specific purpose and mission statement, write them in your own words. Make it so that someone can fully understand what you do here.

Board of Directors

Every nonprofit requires a board of directors. Nonprofits are managed, not owned. Therefore, it is up to the management of the organization to set how things happen. The highest level of management is the board of directors. Although they typically don't handle the day-to-day operations, they legally can. There's nothing legally preventing a board member from being a manager for the ongoing operations. However, if this happens in your organization, you'll have to be cautious to avoid conflicts of interest[19].

Traditionally, the board of directors only handles big decisions. Instead of doing everything themselves, they hire or appoint an executive director to execute their overall mission. That leaves the board to make only bigger directional decisions. For example, the executive director would plan out events and coordinate volunteers. However, the board will pick which of the organization's priorities will receive the most attention.

In this section, you need to specify how many directors there will be, how they get elected, and how they can be removed. Additionally, you should include any specific responsibilities of any board positions here.

Meeting Information

As a North Carolina Nonprofit, you're required to have at least 1 board meeting per year. Personally, I think that is way too few. At a minimum, I think you should have quarterly meetings. The organizations that meet more regularly thrive better than those that have few meetings.

This section is all about when, where, and how you have board meetings. Any special rules about meetings should be in this section. My template is a fairly basic way of handling these.

If you want to allow electronic meetings, proxy voting, or other deviations from in-person meetings, you need to list them here. By default, nonprofits had to meet in person. However, there are actually a lot of potential changes to nonprofit laws[20] in North Carolina coming up! One of those changes is to allow virtual meetings by default.

However, to make your nonprofit covered, you should include any meeting rules you'd like to see.

Executive Team

As mentioned above, the executive team runs the organization on a day-to-day basis. The Board of Directors appoints these positions. This section outlines what executive positions exist, what powers they have, and how they're appointed. Executives only have powers that the board had and gave to them. Therefore, this is the section to outline all of the powers the executives have.

At a minimum, you should list an executive director. This person will be in charge of running the organization like a president or CEO of a for-profit corporation.

If your organization has special requirements for being an officer, this is the section you need to list them. For example, one of the organizations I worked with required that the officers lived or worked in Durham. This helped ensure people were connected to the community.

Additionally, you need to list how the executive team gets appointed and how they can be removed. Typically, I make it so the executives can be appointed and removed by majority vote of the board of directors. That keeps it simple.

Legal Duties & Indemnity

This section is the thickest legalese you'll encounter in all of your nonprofit setup. I combined all the dense stuff in one section on purpose.

First off, I like to specify that directors and officers owe a duty of loyalty[21] and a duty of care[22] as outlined in NCGS §§ 55A-8-30[23] & 42[24].

Secondly, I include a provision limiting the liability of officers and directors as long as they act within their duties of loyalty and care. Most directors are volunteer and most officers aren't paid enough to take on the liabilities of an organization. They shouldn't have to worry about whether they'll be liable in case a decision hurts the organization. It's also good to carry insurance on directors and officers for this same reason.

Thirdly, to help protect your officers and directors, I include an indemnification provision. An indemnification provision basically states that the organization will defend and pay any lawsuit judgment against an officer or director that results from actions they took in their role as officer or director.

Finally, I add a provision that says officers and directors won't be held personally responsible for actions the organization takes. Together, these 3 provisions create the most comprehensive protection you can create in your bylaws for your officers and directors.

Dissolution and Termination

Finally, you need to address dissolution and termination in your bylaws. In this section, you need to specify how and when the organization can dissolve. After that, you need to specify what happens to the organization and the assets in the dissolution process.

If you used my sample Articles of Incorporation, you already have a clause that outlines what happens to the assets during a dissolution. You can repeat that language here or expand upon it. Some people like to specify what charity or causes will be funded in the event of a dissolution.

In my template Bylaws, I copy the language from the articles. You can make this more specific or leave it as is.

Nonprofit Bylaws

That should do it! Your bylaws are ready to be ratified by the board of directors at your first board meeting. You can also add other provisions you'd like to include. Keep in mind that your bylaws are meant to be fairly unchanged year to year. If you want more specific governance decisions, you can always make those changes in board resolutions or through your meeting minutes.

Before your first board meeting, we need to create a conflict of interest policy. That's next.

CONFLICT OF INTEREST POLICY

Every nonprofit needs to adopt a conflict of interest policy. A template copy is available in the exhibits to this book or you can download a copy at the following address: https://nc.business/product/nonprofit-conflict-of-interest-policy/.

North Carolina has a Conflict of Interest law, but it doesn't cover how you should avoid them. Therefore, you need to create one that has a procedure you can follow that also adequately protects your organization.

Our NC.Business template is tried and true. Many of my North Carolina Nonprofit clients have adopted and are using this template in their organization. Not only are they good policy, but this template has been approved by the IRS.

If you're going to apply for 501c3 recognition, you need a Conflict of Interest Policy that the IRS will approve. This is an already approved policy for a North Carolina Nonprofit.

Interested Person

When you're creating your conflict of interest policy for your North Carolina Nonprofit, you first have to define who an interested person is. An interested person is anyone who seeks to gain in any particular decision. It's only ever a problem if an interested person also has control over that decision in any way.

Disclosing Conflicts

To avoid conflicts from harming your organization, you need a policy where all decision makers are required to disclose any potential conflicts. Generally, you should have them disclose directly to the board. However, as organizations grow, you might change that policy to have them disclose to their supervisor or a separate governing body.

Determination of Conflict

Next, you need a method for determining if there actually is a conflict. All directors, officers, managers, and other decision makers need to disclose potential conflicts. However, not all potential conflicts end up being real conflicts.

For example, if a volunteer offers to sell his car to a board member, that board member should disclose the potential conflict. However, it's probably safe to say that this transaction didn't arise from any malice towards the organization. It's important that your team aim for being especially cautious with conflicts of interest.

Addressing the Conflict

Once potential conflicts are reported and the board determines there's actually a conflict, you need a policy for dealing with them. If you're a director in a North Carolina Nonprofit, you have a duty of loyalty and a duty of care to your organization. Therefore, it's your duty to act in the organizations best interest when addressing the conflict of interest.

I prefer to use the following procedures for addressing conflicts:

1. Give the interested person a short opportunity to address the conflict and how that person will uphold their duties and the conflict.
2. Have a discussion without the interested person as well as a vote on what to do.
3. The board should either rule the conflict isn't an issue or make the decision for the interested person.
4. Document everything.

In this policy, documentation is incredibly important. Without documentation, you still have the appearance of impropriety. In most cases, the board will make the decision on behalf of the interested person. That avoids almost all appearance of impropriety.

Penalties

Finally, you need penalties. If a person in your organization acts against the organization's best interests or fails to disclose potential conflicts, he or she is hurting the organization as a whole. It's important to stamp this type of behavior out immediately. Depending on the severity, a person could be written up, suspended, or even terminated for violations of this policy.

Even if the board doesn't use these punishments in all cases, it's important to have them when needed. In my experience, conflicts are more often encountered accidentally than maliciously.

FIRST BOARD MEETING

FIRST BOARD MEETING

Tasks for your First Board Meeting

- ☐ Appoint Your Board
- ☐ Ratify Articles and EIN
- ☐ Ratify Bylaws
- ☐ Enact Conflict of Interest Policy
- ☐ Elect Officers
- ☐ Approve Budget & Past Expenses
- ☐ Create Future Plans

Don't forget to take minutes and set an agenda!

NC.Business

You've done a ton of work already. Unfortunately,

up until your first board meeting, your organization isn't even legally valid yet. The first board meeting is a legal requirement for your North Carolina Nonprofit. It's important and necessary because several key things take place here.

I'm about to throw a lot of tasks at you in a short amount of time. Just make sure you complete everything on this checklist. You might have more based on your immediate needs, but these are the legally required ones.

Appoint Your Board

I've included a template for appointment of the board of directors by the incorporator in the Exhibits of this book.

If you set up the North Carolina Nonprofit, you're in the driver's seat here. Your initial position is called the "Incorporator." As incorporator, you get to appoint the first board of directors. However, if your organization has members, they get to select the board instead of you. Just another great reason to not have members[25].

Fortunately, as incorporator, your process is super simple. You just need to sign a document that says that you, as incorporator, appoint the following people to the board of directors for ABC Corp. It's that easy.

Once they've been appointed, your board needs to

select who will run the meetings. Usually, boards have a chairperson, vice chairperson, and secretary. Your board can decide these positions among themselves. Yes, you can appoint yourself, but be careful because this might create a conflict of interest if you wanted to be executive director.

Ratify Articles & EIN

Next, your new board of directors needs to ratify a few things that you, the incorporator, have done on behalf of the organization. I've included a template to use for your board resolution where you ratify the bylaws, conflict of interest policy, and the expenses paid by the incorporator.

Incorporators have very limited power to act on behalf of a company. Their power basically ends when the bare minimum is completed to set up a company. In the case of a North Carolina Nonprofit, that's the articles, EIN, and a few incidental expenses on the way. For example, it's fine for an incorporator to obtain a domain name, but generally not okay to hire employees.

People should also not want to deal with an incorporator. Unless the board of directors ratifies the incorporator's actions, any contracts that bind the nonprofit are null and void.

However, that doesn't mean everyone can walk away free. Many contracts will then fall to the incorporator to fulfill them.

Let's just get started with the big ones: ratifying the Articles of Incorporation and the EIN. These are the core elements of the organization, so this should be a no-brainer if they were done correctly.

I've supplied the template above that covers a lot of these ratifications in one document.

Ratify Bylaws

Next, your organization needs to ratify and adopt the bylaws. It's pretty common to make a few changes before ratification. Because of that, you should send the bylaws to your chosen board members before the meeting. They need a chance to review all the materials you're sending to them. This is a very intense meeting, and it would be made so much worse if everyone had to make a decision on the bylaws on the spot.

My template above also covers this.

Adopt Conflict of Interest Policy

After that, your board needs to adopt a conflict of interest policy. Whether you're using my template or your own, you should provide it to your directors ahead of time.

Appoint Officers

The remaining items don't have to happen in any

particular order. I prefer to tackle officers next because it just feels right at this juncture. I've included a template for the appointment of officers in the Exhibits of this book.

Your organization needs at least one officer to run the day-to-day operations. You can give this person any title you want. However, most commonly, their title is executive director or president. They can even be the officer and a member of the board of directors, though that can create conflicts[26].

What is important is picking someone who will fulfill their duties and help build the organization. Your bylaws should specify what officers your organization has and how to appoint them.

If you're using my template, be sure to adjust the officers for what positions you have. If you only have an Executive Director, you do not need to appoint a treasurer. Additionally, my template above refers to the positions created in the Template Bylaws of mine, specifically Section 5.8. If you're using different bylaws, you should refer to your officer positions in that part.

Approve Budget & Past Expenses

There are many ways to create a budget. I have a friend who made a great video about creating budgets for nonprofits. Check out Amber Melanie Smith on YouTube [27]for some great videos about nonprofits.

At this stage, you need to create a budget, approve that budget, and decide whether or not the organization will approve past expenses by the incorporator.

If the incorporator is on the board of directors, they cannot vote on whether to reimburse themselves for those past expenses. This is a great example of a conflict of interest. This might not seem fair, but it's how it is. Additionally, I've never seen a board not approve past expenses. However, I've never seen unreasonable expenses by an incorporator either.

I've included a provision for reimbursing the incorporator in my First Board Meetings Resolutions template above.

Create a Game Plan for the Future

Now we're finally to the fun part! Most people agree that planning for the future is a lot more interesting than ratifying bylaws. I'm a lawyer and I even think bylaws are rather boring. They're important to have, but the nonprofit's mission is why nonprofits exist.

Take this opportunity, while you have your board in one place, to generate plans. Use everyone's excitement to put together tentative plans for the future.

Finally, pick your regular meetings for the rest of the year. It's best to get everyone on the same page about how often meetings are and what is expected of them. Your first years are critical for your organization's long term survival. Therefore, you need committed board members.

Don't Forget

Don't forget to take meeting minutes through all of this! Not only are they legally required, they're important for institutional memory. You don't need to make your meeting minutes fancy. I've included a sample template for meeting minutes in the Exhibits.

Additionally, if your incorporator took any other actions before this first meeting, you need to ratify those actions as well. Feel free to add additional items to the resolutions I provided where you see fit. For example, if your incorporator opened a bank account, you need to ratify that. You will also need to change the signatories on that account now that you have a board and an officer!

TIPS FOR MOVING FORWARD

If you've gone through all these steps, you have a legally established North Carolina Nonprofit! That's a very exciting accomplishment. I can't wait to see how your organization will improve the community.

I've compiled a few tips based on what I've seen nonprofits run into.

You cannot ask anyone for donations until you've obtained a solicitation license. It's an easy process we'll cover in a future article.

Donations to your organization are not tax deductible unless and until you obtain 501c3 recognition through the IRS.

Don't forget to file your 990s with the IRS each year. You can lose your status or have your organization dissolved if you don't. Even if you have $0 in revenue, you still need to file.

Keep meeting regularly as a board and keep up the documentation. Good records are necessary for a successful nonprofit.

EXHIBITS

Here you'll find a series of documents referenced throughout this book.

List of Exhibits

1. Articles of Incorporation Nonprofit Corporation
2. Nonprofit Bylaws
3. Conflict of Interest Policy
4. Appointment By Board of Directors by Incorporator
5. Board Resolution of the First Board Meeting
6. Appointment of Officers
7. Meeting Minutes

State of North Carolina
Department of the Secretary of State

ARTICLES OF INCORPORATION
NONPROFIT CORPORATION

Pursuant to §55A-2-02 of the General Statutes of North Carolina, the undersigned corporation does hereby submit these Articles of Incorporation for the purpose of forming a nonprofit corporation.

[DELETE THIS BEFORE FILING] These Articles were drafted by Richard Bobholz of https://NC.Business and are subject to the Terms and Conditions found at https://nc.business/terms-and-conditions/. Any use not authorized in those terms is a violation (and is super easy to track since you're filing with a public database). If you want to modify any version of Nonprofit Articles, you should download the one off the Secretary of State's website and modify them: https://www.sosnc.gov/forms/by_title/_Business_Registration_Business_Entities_Common.

1. The name of the nonprofit corporation is:.
____

2. _____(Check only if applicable.) The corporation is a charitable or religious corporation as defined in NCGS §55A-1-40(4).

3. The name of the initial registered agent is:
____

4. The street address and county of the initial registered agent's office of the corporation is:

Number and Street:______________________________

City:____________ State: NC Zip Code:________County:________

5. The name and address of each incorporator is as follows:
____
____

6.(Check either "a" or "b" below.)

a.___The corporation will have members.

b._x_The corporation will not have members.

7. Distribution of Assets Upon Dissolution. Upon the dissolution of the corporation, the Board of Directors shall, after paying or making provisions for the payment of all of the liabilities of the corporation, dispose of all of the assets of the corporation exclusively for the purposes of the corporation in such manner, or to such organization or organizations organized and operated exclusively for religious, charitable, educational, scientific or literary purposes as shall at the time qualify as an exempt organization or organizations under Section 501(c)(3) of the Code as the Board of Directors shall determine, or to federal, state, or local governments to be used exclusively for public purposes. Any such assets not so disposed of shall be disposed of by the Superior Court of the county in which the principal office of the corporation is then located, exclusively for such purposes or to such organizations, such as the court shall determine, which are organized and operated exclusively for such purposes, or to such governments for such purposes.

8. No Benefit to Members and Directors. No part of the net earnings of the corporation shall inure to the benefit of or be distributable to, its members, directors, officers or other private persons except that the corporation shall be authorized and empowered to pay reasonable compensation for services rendered and to make payments and distributions in furtherance of purposes set forth in these articles of incorporation. No substantial part of the activities of the corporation shall be the carrying on of propaganda or otherwise attempting to influence legislation, and the corporation shall not participate in or intervene in (including the publishing or distribution of statements) any political campaign on behalf of or in opposition to any candidate for public office. Notwithstanding any other provisions of these articles, the corporation shall not carry on any other activities not permitted to be carried on (a) by a corporation exempt from federal income tax under Section 501(c)(3) of the Code or(b) by a corporation, contributions to which are deductible under Section 170(c)(2) of the Code.

9. Conflicts of Interest Policy. The Board of Directors shall adopt a Conflicts of Interest Policy that may change from time to time by written direction of the Board of Directors. However, at a minimum, it shall include provisions that prevent any officer of the corporation from voting on any matter related to his or her employment status, budget, or compensation. All officers and board members shall have a duty to disclose any potential conflicts to the Board of Directors when they're first discovered.

The Board of Directors shall keep a written record of any conflicts of interest and how they were managed.

10. The street address and county of the principal office of the corporation is:

Principal Office Telephone Number:____________________

____

Number and Street:

City:____________ State: _____ Zip Code:_______ County:__________

11. **(Optional):** Listing of Officers:

Name	Address	Title
		Executive Director
		Treasurer
		Secretary
		Board Chairperson

12. These articles will be effective upon filing, unless a future time and/or date is specified: __________________________

This is the___ day of__________________, 20___.

____

Incorporator Business Entity Name

____

Signature of Incorporator

________________________, Incorporator

Type or print Incorporator's name and title, if any

BYLAWS
Of

____

Section 1 General Provisions

1.1 **Name**

The name of the corporation is ______________________. (the "Company").

1.2 **Registered Agent**

The initial registered agent of the Company shall be as listed on the Secretary of State's Website. Such registered agent may change from time to time at the decision of a majority vote of the Board of Directors and will be changed on the Secretary of State's website immediately after any such change.

1.3 **Duration**

The duration of the Company is perpetual.

1.4 **Accounting Method**

The Company shall use a cash basis accounting method with the fiscal year ending June 30th. Any partial year shall be reported as a partial year.

1.5 **Formation**

This Company was formed by filing the Articles of Incorporation with the Secretary of State of North Carolina as a nonprofit Corporation. This Company was formed using the Nonprofit Articles and Bylaws from NC.Business. No attorney advised any person in the drafting or execution of these Bylaws.

1.6 **Modifying or Amending Bylaws**

a) These Bylaws may be amended or modified with a two-thirds vote of all directors currently serving on the Board of Directors.

b) Notice of such a proposed change must be made in writing to each Director more than fourteen (14) days but less than forty-five (45) days prior to the vote. Notice must be actually received or served to the last address on record for that Director. Notice is deemed given three (3) days after being deposited with the United States Postal Service.

1.7 **Choice of Law**

These Bylaws and any action taken in regards to them, or disputes arising out of them, shall be subject to the laws of the State of North Carolina, excluding that State's choice of law principles.

Section 2 Purpose

2.1 **Purpose Generally**

The Company is organized exclusively for charitable, religious, educational, and scientific purposes, including, for such purposes, the making of distributions to organizations that qualify as exempt organizations under 501(c)(3) of the Internal Revenue Code, or corresponding section of any future federal tax code.

2.2 **Purpose Specifically**

The specific purpose of the Company is

____

____

____

____

____

________________________.

2.3 **Powers**

The Company shall have and exercise any and all powers necessary, incidental or desirable to accomplish the foregoing purposes and business, to the extent the same may be legally exercised by corporations under State and Federal law. The Company shall carry out its business and exercise its powers pursuant to the arrangements set forth in the Articles of Incorporation and this Agreement.

2.4 **Mission Statement**

The mission of the Company is

____

____

____.

2.5 **Non-Discrimination Policy**

The Company shall not discriminate against any person on the basis of actual or perceived race, color, religion, national origin, sex, gender, identity, sexual orientation, or disability, in any matter of membership, employment, participation, or policy.

Section 3 Board of Directors

3.1 **Powers of the Board of Directors**

The management powers of the Company shall be vested in the Board of Directors unless specifically granted to an Executive or Officer by these Bylaws or by Board Resolution and such Executive or Officer position is not vacant.

3.2 **Number of Directors**

There shall be no less than three directors and no more than nine serving on the Board of Directors at one time to be affixed by the Board of Directors.

3.3 **Term**

The Directors shall serve one year terms. The Term of the Director shall begin on the day after the Annual Meeting and shall last until a new Director is voted to take his or her place, resignation, termination or death, whichever event happens first.

3.4 **Votes**

Each Director has one vote while sitting on the Board of Directors. Under every circumstance where a vote is necessary, each Director shall cast his or her vote affirmatively or negatively, or he or she may abstain.

3.5 **Voting In Directors**

a) At each Annual Meeting, all Board positions are voted on in an order the Board Chairperson selects. The previous Board continues to serve until the first meeting is called by the new Board Chairperson, which may, and is recommended to, be immediately after the Annual Meeting. Any positions that did not receive a majority vote are vacated.

b) If there are ever less than three Directors, the Board Chairperson, or highest ranking Director, may appoint enough persons to serve the remaining board term that would increase the total number of Directors to three.

(1) For the purpose of this section, the ranking of the Directors shall go in this order: (1) Board Chairperson, (2) Board Vice Chairperson, (3) Board Secretary, (4) All Remaining Directors in order of when that Director was first voted to be a Director in this and any contiguous director terms. (If two directors were voted in at the same Annual Meeting, the Director who was voted in first has seniority)

c) If there is ever a situation where there are zero Directors, the Executive Director, or absent an Executive Director, the longest serving Executive or Officer of the Company, must select three non-related Board Members to serve out the remaining year term.

3.6 **Removal of Directors**

Directors may be removed for cause by a majority vote among the Board of Directors. For cause may include breach of duty of care; breach of duty of loyalty; gross negligence; gross incompetence; being convicted of a felony, any degree of embezzlement, arson, theft or misappropriation; or public conduct which is extraordinarily damaging to the Company as a whole. Directors may be removed for any level of illegal drug use.

a) Directors may be removed for any breach of the Director Contract or for any reason outlined in the Director Contract.

3.7 **Board Positions**

a) **Board Chairperson**
There shall be a Board Chairperson, voted on at the Annual Meeting by the Directors. The Board Chairperson shall have the power, among other things, to call meetings, run the meetings, nominate executives and appoint meeting secretaries. The Board Chairperson makes policies on how meetings are conducted and must ensure that such policies are fair.

b) **Board Vice Chairperson**
There shall be a Board Vice Chairperson, voted on at the Annual Meeting by the Directors. The Board Vice Chairperson shall have the powers of the Board Chairperson should the Board Chairperson be unable or unwilling to perform his or her duties.

c) **Board Secretary**
The Board Secretary, if elected, shall be in charge of any written, or otherwise, communications between the Board of Directors and the Executives, general public and any state requirements.

3.8 **Compensation**

The Board will, by resolution, fix the fees and other compensation for the Directors for their services as Directors, including their services as members of committees of the Board.

a) Any changes to the compensation for the Directors shall not occur retroactively.

b) Any changes to the compensation for the Directors shall occur only after a Director's term has expired. No currently serving Directors may change their own salary for the term for which he or she is serving.

3.9 **Conflict of Interest**

a) All Directors and Officers of the Company shall sign a Conflict of Interest Policy, as determined by the Board of Directors.

Section 4 Meetings

4.1 Annual Meeting

a) A meeting of the Directors will be held annually for the purpose of electing the Directors of the Company and for the purpose of doing other business as may come before the meeting. If the day fixed for the annual meeting is a legal holiday in the State of North Carolina, a weekend, or otherwise generally inconvenient for the Directors, the annual meeting will be held on the next succeeding business day or on a date determined by the Board of Directors for the Company that is no later than two weeks after the date specified in the meeting notice.

b) An annual meeting cannot be adjourned without a majority vote by present Directors. The Board Chairperson, or acting Chairperson, may adjourn the meeting without a vote in emergency situations.

4.2 Regular Meeting

The Board of Directors shall have regular quarterly meetings to discuss the regular operations of the Company.

a) Notice Required: Notice of at least fourteen (14) days must be given prior to a Board Meeting to each

Director. This notice may be waived if all Directors agree to waive the notice requirement.

b) Quorum: In order for a vote to be called, a Board Meeting must have a majority of Directors present or present via electronic means, proxy or voting trust.

4.3 Place of Meeting

The place of each meeting will be decided by the Board Chairperson, but the place must be reasonably accessible for all Directors.

4.4 Time and Date of Meeting

The time and date of each meeting will be decided by the Board Chairperson, but the time and place must be reasonable. Such a determination must not be made with the intent to exclude any Director or group of Directors.

4.5 Electronic Meetings

a) "Remote Communication" means any electronic communication including conference telephone, video conference, the Internet, or any other method currently available or developed in the future by which Directors not present in the same physical location may simultaneously communicate with each other.

b) A meeting of the Board may be held by any means of Remote Communication by which all persons authorized to vote or take other action at the meeting has a reasonable opportunity to participate. This remote participation in a meeting will constitute presence in person at the meeting.

4.6 Meeting Conduct

a) Meetings shall be conducted professionally and in accordance with the Roberts Rules of Order or other similar agreed upon method of conducting the meetings.

b) Minutes shall be kept at all meetings of the Directors regardless of quorum or actions taken.

4.7 Proxy Voting and Voting Trusts

Directors may vote by means of a proxy or voting trust, but any voting arrangement does not absolve a Director of his or her duties to the Company. Regardless of voting arrangement, each Director is fully responsible for his or her vote and the duty to be fully informed prior to the vote on each issue.

4.8 Bond

No bond shall be required by any Director.

4.9 Insurance

The Company shall obtain liability insurance for its Directors.

4.10 Actions of Board Without a Meeting

The Board of Directors may take any action consistent with the powers provided to the Board of Directors if written consent is obtained by two thirds majority of the Directors. Such action must be signed by the number of Directors sufficient to take that action at an actual meeting under the terms of this Agreement. This section applies to any vote that requires a Board Meeting with or without quorum except the Annual Meeting.

4.11 Specific Powers Unable to be Delegated

a) **Approval of Annual Budget.** The Board of Directors is responsible for requesting and approving the annual budget for the Company. The Board of Directors may request an officer, CPA, agent of the Company or other qualified person to compile the annual budget prior to the Board of Directors approving it.

b) **Appointment of Executives.** The Board of Directors is solely responsible for appointing the Executive Officers or highest-level Managers of the Company.

c) **Election of Directors.** The Board of Directors is the only entity that may vote in the selection of Directors unless there is, at any point in time, zero Directors in the Board of Directors. If there is ever a situation where there are zero Directors, the Board of Directors shall be repopulated as outlined in Section 3.5 above.

d) **Annual Meeting and Corporate Formalities.** The Board of Directors is solely responsible for ensuring an annual meeting is conducted, annual reports are filed, and any state or federally required formalities are followed.

Section 5 Executive Team

5.1 Powers

The Board of Directors has the authority to appoint members of the Executive Team (the "Officers" or "Executives") to carry out the day-to-day operations of the Company. The powers of the Officer must be explicitly designated in writing and may not exceed the power originally vested in the Board of Directors.

a) The Board of Directors may delegate certain powers to be exclusively carried out by a particular officer. In that case, the Board of Directors no longer has the power to carry out that activity unless there is no officer in that position.

5.2 Vote Required

Any member of the Executive team must be voted in by a majority vote at any Board Meeting with quorum.

5.3 Removal

Any member of the Executive team may be removed by a majority vote at any Board Meeting with quorum. Reason for removal must be recorded in writing in the file for that Officer.

5.4 Duty of Loyalty

Officers of the Company have a Duty of Loyalty and may not engage in business transactions that are in conflict with the Company, engage in conduct that harms the company, or engage in conduct that the Officer knew or should have known has a substantial likelihood, from a reasonable person's view, of harming the Company.

5.5 Duty of Care

Officers of the Company have a Duty of Care and must conduct themselves reasonably in order to ensure that the Officer is not acting or omitting in a manner that he or she knew or should have known would cause harm to the Company. Officers may mitigate this requirement by seeking counsel from a competent person who is capable of providing professional advice on a particular decision prior to making the decision.

Officers in violation of this section may be held liable to the Company for the damage they cause, subject to the decision of the Board of Directors.

5.6 Oath of Office

If the Board of Directors so chooses, an Officer may be required to give an Oath/Affirmation of Office so long as such an Oath/Affirmation does not conflict with that Officer's personal, cultural, or religious beliefs.

5.7 Personal Use

Officers are not permitted to use Company resources for personal use or personal gain unless such personal use of Company property is part of a duly authorized compensation package.

5.8 Executive Positions

Although the Board is not required to use these particular positions, and may design positions aside from these, the positions listed in this section are pre-defined and any reference to these titles is a reference to the rights and responsibilities listed herein.

a) **Executive Director**

The Board of Directors may appoint an "Executive Director." The Executive Director is the principal executive officer of the Company and subject to the control of the Board of Directors, shall in general supervise and control all of the business and affairs of the Company. He or she shall take action on behalf of the Company with respect to all its rights in and to its Subsidiaries and other assets, including casting all votes to which the Company is entitled by nature of its ownership of equity or debt securities. He shall sign any deeds, mortgages, bonds, contracts, or other instruments authorized under this Agreement generally or by the Board of Directors specifically, and in general he shall perform all duties incident to the office of Executive Director and such other duties as may be prescribed by the Board of Directors from time to time.

b) **Treasurer**

The Board of Directors may appoint a Treasurer. The Treasurer shall perform such duties in connection with the long-term financial plan and compliance for the Company as is from time to time determined by the Board of Directors or Executive Director. The Treasurer shall report directly to the Executive Director. The Treasurer shall, when requested, counsel with and advise the other officers of the Corporation and shall perform such other duties as may be requested by the Executive Director or as the Board of Directors may from time to time determine.

c) **Appointments**

(1) The Executive Director may appoint other employees and officers, so long as the authority

granted to those employees or officers does not exceed that of the Executive Director.

(2) The Executive Director may hire and fire employees as needed to carry out the Executive Director's duties. The salary, or other compensation, must be approved by the Board of Directors, unless the monies have been allocated in the approved budget.

Section 6 Fiduciary Duties; Limitation of Liability; Indemnity

6.1 Fiduciary Duties of Directors and Officers

All Directors and Officers of the Company owe to the Company all fiduciary duties set forth in Sections 55A-8-30 and 55A-8-42 of the North Carolina General Statutes as well as any other statutorily required or agreed upon duties for Directors and Officers of a North Carolina Nonprofit Corporation.

6.2 Limitation of Liability

Except as otherwise provided in this Agreement, no Director or Officer of the Company shall be liable to the Company for monetary damages for an act or omission in such Person's capacity as a Director or Officer, except for (i) acts or omissions which such Person knew, at the time of the acts or omissions, were clearly in conflict with the interests of the Company, (ii) any transaction from which such Person derived an improper personal benefit, (iii) acts or omissions occurring prior to the date this provision becomes effective, or (iv) breach of this Agreement or of any contract between the Company and such Person. In addition, the Disinterested Directors, by majority vote, may waive any such claim against a Director or Officer. Any amendment of this Agreement or of the Act subsequent to the date hereof which deletes or modifies the indemnity provided by this Section shall not adversely affect the rights existing at the time of such deletion or modification.

6.3 Indemnification

The Company hereby agrees to indemnify and hold harmless any Person (each an "Indemnified Person") to the fullest extent permitted under the Act, as the same now exists or may hereafter be amended, substituted or replaced (but, in the case of any such amendment, substitution or replacement only to the extent that such amendment, substitution or replacement permits the Company to provide broader indemnification rights than the Company is providing immediately prior to such amendment), against all expenses, liabilities and losses (including attorney fees, judgments, fines, excise taxes or penalties) reasonably incurred or suffered by such Person (or one or more of such Person's Affiliates) by reason of the fact that such Person is or was serving as a Director or Officer of the Company or is or was serving at the request of the Company as a manager, officer, director or member of another partnership, corporation, joint venture, limited liability company, trust or other enterprise; provided, however, that (unless the Board of Directors otherwise consents) no Indemnified Person shall be indemnified for any expenses, liabilities and losses suffered that are attributable to such Indemnified Person's or its Affiliates' gross negligence, willful misconduct or knowing violation of law, actions in bad faith or not done with the reasonable belief that such actions were in the best interests of the Company, or for any losses incurred by the Company. Expenses, including attorney fees, incurred by any such Indemnified Person in defending a proceeding shall be paid by the Company in advance of the final disposition of such proceeding, including any appeal therefrom, upon receipt of an undertaking by or on behalf of such Indemnified Person to repay such amount if it shall ultimately be determined that such Indemnified Person is not entitled to be indemnified by the Company.

6.4 Notice

Any indemnification of or advance of expenses to an Indemnified Person in accordance with Section 6.3 above shall be reported periodically in writing in the Corporate books which are open to inspection, but in any case, within the twelve month period immediately following the date of the indemnification or advance.

6.5 No Personal Liability

Notwithstanding anything contained herein to the contrary (including in this Section 6), any indemnity by the Company relating to the matters covered in this Section 6 shall be provided out of and to the extent of Company assets only and no Director shall have personal liability on account thereof or shall be required to make additional Capital Contributions to help satisfy such indemnity of the Company.

6.6 Personal Guarantee of Company Debts

No Director or Officer is required to provide a personal guarantee on any Company debts. Unless specifically noted in the instrument creating the debt and signed by the Director or Officer to be bound in a personal capacity, there is an assumption of no personal guarantee of any Company debts.

6.7 Loans from Directors or Officers

Upon approval of the terms thereof by the Board of Directors, any Director or Officer may make a loan to the

Company upon commercially reasonable terms, with interest not to exceed 5% per annum.

6.8 Loans to Directors or Officers

The Company shall not make any loans, for any length of time, to any Directors or Officers for any reason.

Section 7 Dissolution and Termination

7.1 Dissolution

a) The Board of Directors may choose to wind up or dissolve the Company upon receipt of a two thirds majority vote and must show good cause in doing so.

b) The Company may dissolve upon Court Order.

7.2 Distribution of Assets Upon Dissolution

Upon the dissolution of the corporation, the Board of Directors shall, after paying or making provisions for the payment of all of the liabilities of the corporation, dispose of all of the assets of the corporation exclusively for the purposes of the corporation in such manner, or to such organization or organizations organized and operated exclusively for religious, charitable, educational, scientific or literary purposes as shall at the time qualify as an exempt organization or organizations under Section 501(c)(3) of the Code as the Board of Directors shall determine, or to federal, state, or local governments to be used exclusively for public purposes. Any such assets not so disposed of shall be disposed of by the Superior Court of the county in which the principal office of the corporation is then located, exclusively for such purposes or to such organizations, such as the court shall determine, which are organized and operated exclusively for such purposes, or to such governments for such purposes.

7.3 Distributions in Kind

As it may not be completely reasonable to sell all the assets, if creditors accept it, distributions in kind may be made to the creditors of the Company. Additionally, distributions in kind may be made to any entity receiving distributions from the dissolution of the Company.

Ratified on this the ____ day of
__________________________, 20___.

____
Signature of Secretary

____
Print Name

[NC.Business Template]

Conflict of Interest Policy

This Conflict of Interest Policy was created by NC.Business and was not created or modified by an attorney. There is no attorney-client relationship between NC.Business and the Organization.

Article I Purpose

The purpose of the Conflict of Interest policy is to protect this tax-exempt organization's (the "Organization") interest when it is contemplating entering into a transaction or arrangement that might benefit the private interest of an officer or director of the Organization or might result in a possible excess benefit transaction. This policy is intended to supplement but not replace any applicable state and federal laws governing Conflict of Interest applicable to nonprofit and charitable organizations.

Article II Definitions

2.01 Interested Person

Any director, principal officer, or member of a committee with governing board delegated powers, who has a direct or indirect financial interest, as defined below, is an interested person.

2.02 Disinterested Person

A person is a Disinterested Person if they have no Financial Interest in a particular decision and no immediate family member or business partner has a Financial Interest in that decision.

2.03 Financial Interest

A person has a financial interest if the person has, directly or indirectly, through business, investment, or family:

a) An ownership or investment interest in any entity with which the Organization has a transaction or arrangement,
b) A compensation arrangement with the Organization or with any entity or individual with which the Organization has a transaction or arrangement, or
c) A potential ownership or investment interest in, or compensation arrangement with, any entity or individual with which the Organization is negotiating a transaction or arrangement.

Compensation includes direct and indirect remuneration as well as gifts or favors that are not insubstantial.

A financial interest is not necessarily a conflict of interest. Under Article III, Section 2, a person who has a financial interest may have a conflict of interest only if the appropriate governing board or committee decides that a conflict of interest exists.

2.04 Governing Board

"Governing Board" shall mean the Board of Directors of the Organization.

Article III Procedures

3.01 Duty to Disclose

In connection with any actual or possible conflict of interest, an Interested Person must disclose the existence of the Financial Interest and be given the opportunity to disclose all material facts to the directors and members of committees with governing board delegated powers considering the proposed transaction or arrangement.

3.02 Determining Whether a Conflict of Interest Exists

After disclosure of the Financial Interest and all material facts, and after any discussion with the Interested Person, he/she shall leave the governing board or committee meeting while the determination of a Conflict of Interest is discussed and voted upon. The remaining board or committee members shall decide if a Conflict of Interest exists.

3.03 Procedures for Addressing the Conflict of Interest

a) An Interested Person may make a presentation at the governing board or committee meeting, but after the presentation, he/she shall leave the meeting during the discussion of, and the vote on, the transaction or arrangement involving the possible Conflict of Interest.
b) The chairperson of the governing board or committee shall, if appropriate, appoint a Disinterested Person or committee to investigate alternatives to the proposed transaction or arrangement.
c) After exercising due diligence, the governing board or committee shall determine whether the Organization can obtain with reasonable efforts a more advantageous transaction or arrangement from a person or entity that would not give rise to a Conflict of Interest.
d) If a more advantageous transaction or arrangement is not reasonably possible under circumstances not producing a Conflict of Interest, the governing board or committee shall determine by a majority vote of the disinterested directors whether the transaction or arrangement is in the Organization's best interest, for its own benefit, and whether it is fair and reasonable. In conformity with the above determination, it shall make its decision as to whether to enter into the transaction or arrangement.

3.04 Violations of the Conflicts of Interest Policy

a) If the governing board or committee has reasonable cause to believe a member, officer, or director has failed to disclose actual or possible Conflicts of Interest, it shall inform that person of the basis for such belief and afford that person an opportunity to explain the alleged failure to disclose.
b) If, after hearing the member, director, or officer's response and after making further investigation as warranted by the circumstances, the governing board or committee determines that person has failed to disclose an actual or possible Conflict of

Interest, it shall take appropriate disciplinary and corrective action.

Article IV Records of Proceedings

The minutes of the governing board and all committees with board delegated powers shall contain:

a) The names of the persons who disclosed or otherwise were found to have a Financial Interest in connection with an actual or possible Conflict of Interest, the nature of the Financial Interest, any action taken to determine whether a Conflict of Interest was present, and the governing board's or committee's decision as to whether a Conflict of Interest in fact existed.
b) The names of the persons who were present for discussions and votes relating to the transaction or arrangement, the content of the discussion, including any alternatives to the proposed transaction or arrangement, and a record of any votes taken in connection with the proceedings.

Article V Compensation

5.01 No Vote on Compensation.

A voting member of the governing board who receives compensation, directly or indirectly, from the Organization for services is precluded from voting on matters pertaining to that member's compensation.

5.02 Member Compensation.

A voting member of any committee whose jurisdiction includes compensation matters and who receives compensation, directly or indirectly, from the Organization for services is precluded from voting on matters pertaining to that member's compensation.

5.03 No Information.

No voting member of the governing board or any committee whose jurisdiction includes compensation matters and who receives compensation, directly or indirectly, from the Organization, either individually or collectively, is prohibited from providing information to any committee regarding compensation.

Article VI Annual Statements

Each director, principal officer and member of a committee with governing board delegated powers shall annually sign a statement which affirms such person:

a) Has received a copy of the conflicts of interest policy,
b) Has read and understands the policy,
c) Has agreed to comply with the policy, and
d) Understands the Organization is charitable and in order to maintain its federal tax exemption it must engage primarily in activities which accomplish one or more of its tax-exempt purposes.

Article VII Periodic Reviews

To ensure the Organization operates in a manner consistent with charitable purposes and does not engage in activities that could jeopardize its tax-exempt status, periodic reviews shall be conducted. The periodic reviews shall, at a minimum, include the following subjects:

a) Whether compensation arrangements and benefits are reasonable, based on competent survey information, and the result of arm's length bargaining.
b) Whether partnerships, joint ventures, and arrangements with management organizations conform to the Organization's written policies, are properly recorded, reflect reasonable investment or payments for goods and services, further charitable purposes and do not result in inurement, impermissible private benefit or in an excess benefit transaction.

Article VIII Use of Outside Experts

When conducting the periodic reviews as provided for in Article VII, the Organization may, but need not, use outside advisors. If outside experts are used, their use shall not relieve the governing board of its responsibility for ensuring periodic reviews are conducted

By our signatures as proof below, this Conflict of Interest Policy was adopted unanimously by the Board of Directors of ________________________________ on this the ____ day of _____________, 20___.

______________________________	______________________________
Chair	Other Officer
______________	______________
Date	Date

Appointment of Board of Directors by Incorporator

I, the undersigned sole Incorporator of ____ (the "Organization"), a North Carolina Nonprofit Corporation, do hereby appoint the following persons as the initial directors on the board of directors for the Organization:

Name	Address

Their appointments shall start immediately upon the date affixed below.

I make this appointment under my authority as Incorporator of the Organization, and I represent and warrant that there are no members of the Organization whose consent I need to make these appointments.

I take this action on this the ____ day of _____________, 20___.

____

Signature

____

Print Name

Board Resolution
Of the First Board Meeting

MAY IT BE RESOLVED, that on this the __ day of ____________________, 20___, we, the board of directors for __________________________ (the "Organization") did meet and unanimously ratified the following actions taken by ______________________(the "Incorporator"):

1. Drafting and filing the Articles of Incorporation with the North Carolina Secretary of State.
2. Obtaining an Employer Identification Number ("EIN") through the Internal Revenue Service ("IRS").
3. The appointment of the Initial Board Members.

MAY IT BE RESOLVED, that on this same day, we have unanimously ratified the Bylaws of the Organization, and by affixing the signature of the Board Secretary to them, we have adopted those Bylaws and shall keep them in the Organization's records.

MAY IT BE RESOLVED, that on this same day, we have unanimously ratified the Conflict of Interest Policy for the Organization, and by affixing the signatures of the Board Chairperson and the Board Secretary to them, we have adopted that Conflict of Interest Policy for the Organization and shall keep them in the Organization's records.

MAY IT BE RESOLVED, that on this the same day, we have unanimously ratified the expenses personally paid by the Incorporator that are attached to this Board Resolution, and unanimously approve the reimbursement of Incorporator immediately when funds become available to do so.

Resolved on the date first listed above.

Board Chairperson	**Board Secretary**
______________________	______________________
Signature	Signature
______________________	______________________
Print Name	Print Name

Appointment of Officers

MAY IT BE RESOLVED, that on this the ___ day of ____________________, 20___, we, the board of directors for ____________________________________(the "Organization") did meet and voted to elect the following persons for the corresponding officer positions, with those powers and responsibilities created in the Bylaws of the Organization Section 5.8.

Name	Address	Officer Position
		Executive Director
		Treasurer

Resolved on the date first listed above.

Board Chairperson

____
Signature

____
Print Name

Board Secretary

____
Signature

____
Print Name

Meeting Minutes

Date & Time:
Location:
Attendees:

-

<u>**Call to Order**</u>: The meeting was called to order at _________ by _____________________ (the Board Chairperson).

1. Approval of Agenda. This Agenda was unanimously approved by the Board of Directors with no alterations or issue.
2. Issue 1
3. Issue 2
4. Issue 3
5. Issue 4
6. New Business
7. Issues Tabled for Next Meeting

<u>**Adjournment**</u>. The meeting was adjourned at ______________ by the Board Chairperson.

Minutes Approved By: **Board Chairperson**	**Minutes Prepared By:** **Board Secretary**
______________________ Signature	______________________ Signature
______________________ Print Name	______________________ Print Name

ABOUT THE AUTHOR

Richard Bobholz is a small business and nonprofit attorney located in Durham, North Carolina. He's been practicing law as the managing attorney and founder of Law++ since 2012 where he works tirelessly to make the legal system easier and more approachable for other business owners. Beyond practicing law, Richard enjoys running, swimming, hiking, playing video games, and most importantly, spending time with his wife and newborn daughter.

Because he works almost exclusively with small business owners and nonprofits, he puts out resources such as this as often as he can. If you need support outside these guides, please feel free to get in touch through www.lawplusplus.com or schedule an appointment through https://calendly.com/lawplusplus.

REFERENCES

---

[1] https://nc.business/2021/11/03/difference-between-a-for-profit-and-a-nonprofit/
[2] https://nc.business/2021/11/10/difference-between-a-nonprofit-and-a-charity/
[3] https://nc.business/2021/10/27/naming-guidelines-for-north-carolina-companies/
[4] https://sosnc.gov/online_services/search/by_title/_Business_Registration
[5] https://nc.business/2020/03/26/what-is-a-dba/
[6] http://tmsearch.uspto.gov/bin/gate.exe?f=login&p_lang=english&p_d=trmk
[7] https://nc.business/2021/11/17/levels-of-trademark-names/
[8] https://www.sosnc.gov/online_services/search/by_title/_trademarks
[9] https://www.sosnc.gov/forms/by_title/_Business_Registration_Business_Entities_Common
[10] https://nc.business/2021/11/20/what-is-a-registered-agent/
[11] https://nc.business/2021/09/08/what-is-limited-liability/
[12] https://paintcoveredoveralls.com/2020/05/10/what-is-an-hoa/
[13] https://nc.business/2021/11/20/what-is-a-conflict-of-interest/
[14] https://nc.business/2021/11/26/what-do-i-do-if-my-articles-get-rejected/
[15] https://nc.business/2020/02/12/how-much-should-i-pay-for-an-ein/
[16] https://nc.business/2020/02/12/get-a-free-ein/
[17] https://www.irs.gov/businesses/small-businesses-self-employed/apply-for-an-employer-identification-number-ein-online
[18] https://nc.business/2020/03/26/what-is-a-dba/

---

[19] https://nc.business/2021/11/20/what-is-a-conflict-of-interest/
[20] https://www.ncnonprofits.org/content/modernizing-north-carolinas-nonprofit-laws
[21] https://nc.business/2021/11/06/duty-of-loyalty/
[22] https://nc.business/2021/11/07/duty-of-care/
[23] https://www.ncleg.gov/EnactedLegislation/Statutes/PDF/BySection/Chapter_55A/GS_55A-8-30.pdf
[24] https://www.ncleg.gov/EnactedLegislation/Statutes/PDF/BySection/Chapter_55A/GS_55A-8-42.pdf
[25] https://www.youtube.com/watch?v=2bxREvONT7Q
[26] https://nc.business/2021/12/08/can-i-be-executive-director-and-a-board-member/
[27] https://www.youtube.com/c/AmberMelanieSmith

Made in United States
Troutdale, OR
11/03/2026

56845100R00056